HOW A KID
SHOULD GROW

Selections from

ne Living Bible

Tyndale House
Publishers, Inc.
Wheaton, Illinois

All Scripture passages are from <u>The Living Bible</u>, paraphrased by Kenneth N. Taylor, ©1971 by Tyndale House Publishers.

STRETCH
First printing, October 1983
Library of Congress Catalog Card Number 83-50480
ISBN 0-8423-6668-7, boys
ISBN 0-8423-6673-3, girls
Copyright © 1983 by Tyndale House Publishers, Inc.
Wheaton, Illinois
Printed in the United States of America

Welcome to the Stretch Squad!

Stretch Squad readers like the idea of growing, of stretching, of exploring new vistas. That's what this book is all about! As you read through *Stretch*—a page each day—you will learn that each book of the Bible has its own special way of explaining how God is able to stretch people just like yourself. *Keep these thoughts ever in mind. They will mean real life for you.* (Proverbs 4:21).

By the end of the year, you will have a good overview of what the Bible says, book by book, beginning with Genesis, where life began, and ending with Revelation where we learn that the time is coming when the whole earth will stagger like a drunkard.

At the end of this book we've left some blank pages—one for each month. Use these pages to record milestones: your first date, birthdays of your family and friends, verses that become special to you as you read through *Stretch*, answers to prayer and so on.

There's also room on most pages for you to record how you feel about what you have read. It's good to underline verses that you particularly like.

We hope *Stretch* will become a special book for you. If so, write and tell us.

Remember, *Stretch* is God's Word. Treat it with reverence. Make it a real part of your day.

Whatever God says to us is full of living power.

Open my eyes to see wonderful things in your Word. I am but a pilgrim here on earth. How I need a map and your commands are my chart and guide.

Your words are a flashlight to light the path ahead of me and keep me from stumbling.

Lord, don't let me make a mess of things. Just tell me what to do and I will do it, Lord. As long as I live I'll wholeheartedly obey. Make me walk along the right paths for I know how delightful they really are.

Hebrews 4:12.
Psalm 119:18,19,105,31,33-35.

GENESIS

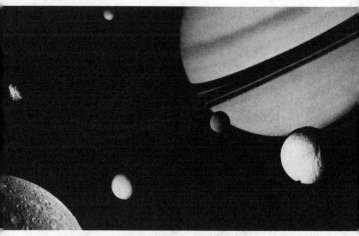

Let everything he has made give praise to him.

Praise him who made the heavens...Praise him who planted the water within the earth...Praise him who made the heavenly lights....the sun to rule the day...and the moon and stars at night.

He merely spoke, and the heavens were formed, and all the galaxies of stars. He made the oceans, pouring them into his vast reservoirs. For when he but spoke, the world began! It appeared at his command!

The clouds are his chariots. He rides upon the wings of the wind.

Praise God forever! How he must rejoice in all his work. The earth trembles at his glance. The mountains burst into flame at his touch.

Psalm 148:5. Psalm 136:5-9. Psalm 33:6,7,9. Psalm 104:3,31,32.

The earth was at first a shapeless, chaotic mass.

Before the mountains were created, before the earth was formed, you are God without beginning or end.

You laid the foundations of the earth, and made the heavens with your hands!

You alone are God. You have made the skies and the heavens, the earth and the seas, and everything in them. You preserve it all. And all the angels of heaven worship you.

O Lord, you have reigned from prehistoric times, from the everlasting past. The majesty and glory of your name fills all the earth and overflows the heavens.

You do such wonderful things!

Genesis 1:2. Psalm 90:2. Psalm 102:25.
Nehemiah 9:6. Psalm 93:2. Psalm 8:1. Isaiah 25:1.

GENESIS

**The
Lord God
formed a
man's body
from the
dust of the ground
and breathed into it the
breath of life, and man
became a living person.**

The Lord gazes down upon mankind
from heaven where he lives. He has
made their hearts and closely watches
everything they do. He created all the
people of the world from one man,
Adam, and scattered the nations across
the face of the earth. He decided
beforehand which should rise and
fall, and when. He determined
their boundaries. His purpose in
all of this is that they
should seek after God,
and perhaps feel their
way toward him and
find him—though he
is not far from any
one of us. For in him
we live and move
and are!

Genesis 2:7. Psalm 33:13-15.
Acts 17:26-28.

They heard the sound of the Lord God walking in the garden...
"Why are you hiding?"

And Adam replied, "I heard you coming and didn't want you to see me naked. So I hid."

"Who told you you were naked?" the Lord God asked. "Have you eaten fruit from the tree I warned you about?"

"Yes," Adam admitted, "but it was the woman you gave me who brought me some, and I ate it."

A man who refuses to admit his mistakes can never be successful. But if he confesses and forsakes them, he gets another chance.

He (God) can be depended on to forgive us and to cleanse us from every wrong. And it is perfectly proper for God to do this for us because Christ died to wash away our sins.

Genesis 3:8-12. Proverbs 28:13. 1 John 1:9.

GENESIS

Noah was a pleasure to the Lord.

He was the only truly righteous man living on the earth at that time. He tried always to conduct his affairs according to God's will.

There lived in the land of Uz a man named Job—a good man who feared God and stayed away from evil.

Look at the Lord's prophets. We know how happy they are now because they stayed true to him then, even though they suffered greatly for it.

These people all trusted God and as a result won battles, overthrew kingdoms, ruled their people well, and received what God had promised them.

Genesis 6:8-10. Job 1:1. James 5:10,11. Hebrews 11:33.

GENESIS

We started out bad, being born with evil natures, and were under God's anger just like everyone else.

The people who lived there began to talk about building a great city, with a temple-tower reaching to the skies—a proud, eternal monument to themselves.

God scattered them all over the earth. And that ended the building of the city.

Ever since man was first placed upon the earth, the triumph of the wicked has been short-lived, and the joy of the godless but for a moment. Though the godless be proud as the heavens, and walk with his nose in the air, yet he shall perish forever.

Because of (God's) kindness you have been saved through trusting Christ. And even trusting is not of yourselves; it too is a gift from God. Salvation is not a reward for the good we have done, so none of us can take any credit for it.

Ephesians 2:3. Genesis 11:3,4,8. Job 20:4-7. Ephesians 2:8,9.

GENESIS

Esau hated Jacob.

As the boys grew, Esau became a skillful hunter, while Jacob was a quiet sort who liked to stay at home.

Isaac's favorite was Esau . . . and Rebekah's favorite was Jacob.

A man's enemies will be found in his own home. Brothers will betray each other.

But that isn't the way Christ taught you! Stop being mean, bad-tempered and angry. Quarreling, harsh words, and dislike of others should have no place in your lives.

Instead, be kind to each other, tenderhearted, forgiving one another.

Genesis 27:41. Genesis 25:27, 28. Micah 7:6. Mark 13:12. Ephesians 4:20, 31, 32.

God turned into good what you meant for evil.

When the traders came by, his brothers pulled Joseph out of the well and sold him to them for twenty pieces of silver, and they took him along to Egypt.

When Joseph arrived in Egypt...everything he did succeeded. Pharaoh said to him, "You are the wisest man in the country!"

 Pharaoh placed his own signet ring on Joseph's finger as a token of his authority, and dressed him in beautiful clothing and placed the royal golden chain about his neck and declared, "See, I have placed you in charge of all the land of Egypt."

Happy are those who are persecuted because they are good, for the Kingdom of Heaven is theirs. All that happens to us is working for our good if we love God and are fitting into his plans.

Genesis 50:20. Genesis 37:28. Genesis 39:1,2. Genesis 41:39,41.
Matthew 5:10. Romans 8:28.

EXODUS

Praise the God who...brought his people safely out of Egypt.

Praise the Lord who opened the Red Sea to make a path before them...and led them safely through...but drowned Pharaoh's army in the sea. Praise him who led his people through the wilderness.

The Red Sea saw them coming and quickly broke apart before them. The Jordan River opened up a path for them to cross.

He remembered our utter weakness. And saved us from our foes. He gives food to every living thing.

Oh, give thanks to the God of heaven, for his lovingkindness continues.

Psalm 136:10. Psalm 105:37. Psalm 136:13-16. Psalm 114:3. Psalm 136:23-26.

EXODUS

The Lord said to Moses, " . . . I have appointed you as my ambassador."

"But I'm not the person for a job like that!" Moses exclaimed. "I'm just not a good speaker. I never have been, and I'm not now, even after you have spoken to me, for I have a speech impediment."

"Who makes mouths?" Jehovah asked him. "Isn't it I, the Lord? Who makes a man so that he can speak or not speak, see or not see, hear or not hear?"

There has never been another prophet like Moses, for the Lord talked to him face to face. And at God's command he performed amazing miracles which have never been equaled.

Exodus 7:1. Exodus 3:11. Exodus 4:10,11. Deuteronomy 34:11,12.

EXODUS

The people of Israel multiplied explosively until they were a greater nation than their rulers.

So the Egyptians made slaves of them and put brutal taskmasters over them. The Israelis were groaning beneath their burdens, in deep trouble because of their slavery, and weeping bitterly before the Lord. He heard their cries from heaven.

The Lord replied, "I will arise and defend the oppressed, the poor, the needy. I will rescue them as they have longed for me to do."

By means of many remarkable miracles he led them out of Egypt and through the Red Sea.

The Lord is still in his holy temple. He still rules from heaven. He closely watches everything that happens here on earth. He shines forever without change or shadow.

Psalm 105:24. Exodus 1:11. Exodus 2:23.
Psalm 12:5. Acts 7:36. Psalm 11:4.
James 1:17.

EXODUS

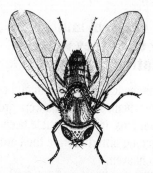

**The Egyptians will find out
that I am indeed God
when I show them
my power and force them
to let my people go.**

The river turned to blood. Frogs covered the nation. Lice
infected the entire nation. There were terrible swarms of
flies. All the cattle of the Egyptians began dying. Boils
broke out. Thunder and hail and lightning. All Egypt lay
in ruins. Locusts covered the face of the earth. There
remained not one green thing—not a tree, not a plant.
Thick darkness over all the land. At midnight, Jehovah
killed all the firstborn sons...and there was bitter crying.

So he brought his chosen ones singing into the
Promised Land. He gave them the lands of the Gentiles,
complete with their growing crops. They ate what others
planted. Egypt was glad when they were gone, for the
dread of them was great.

For good men the path is not uphill and rough!
God...smooths the road before them.

Exodus 7:5,20. Exodus 8:6,17,24. Exodus 9:6,10,23,25. Exodus 10:15,22.
Exodus 12:29,30. Psalm 105:43,44,38. Isaiah 26:7.

EXODUS

The Lord guided them by a pillar of cloud during the daytime, and by a pillar of fire at night.

God did not lead them through the land of the Philistines, although that was the most direct route from Egypt to the Promised Land. Instead, God led them along a route through the Red Sea wilderness.

This plan of mine is not what you would work out, neither are my thoughts the same as yours! For just as the heavens are higher than the earth, so are my ways higher than yours, and my thoughts than yours.

This great God is our God forever and ever. He will be our guide until we die.

Exodus 13:21,17,18. Isaiah 55:8,9.
Psalm 48:14.

EXODUS

These are the laws of Jehovah. / Those who... obey them shall be great in the Kingdom of Heaven.

 YOU MAY WORSHIP NO OTHER GOD THAN ME. / Worship only the Lord God. Obey only him.

 YOU SHALL NOT MAKE YOURSELVES ANY IDOLS. / There is only one God, the Father, who created all things and made us to be his own.

 YOU SHALL NOT USE THE NAME OF JEHOVAH YOUR GOD IRREVERENTLY. / Don't make any vows! Your word is enough.

 OBSERVE THE SABBATH AS A HOLY DAY. / Let us not neglect our church meetings, as some people do. The Sabbath was made to benefit man.

 HONOR YOUR FATHER AND MOTHER. / God has put them in authority over you. If you honor your father and mother, yours will be a long life, full of blessing.

Exodus 35:1. Matthew 5:19. Exodus 20:3. Matthew 4:10. Exodus 20:4. 1 Corinthians 8:6. Exodus 20:7. Matthew 5:34,37. Exodus 20:8. Hebrews 10:25. Mark 2:27. Exodus 20:12. Ephesians 6:1,3.

YOU MUST NOT MURDER. / I (Christ) have added to that rule, and tell you that if you are only angry, even in your own home, you are in danger of judgment!

YOU MUST NOT COMMIT ADULTERY. / God has not called us to be dirty-minded...but to be holy and clean.

YOU MUST NOT STEAL. / If anyone is stealing he must stop it and begin using those hands of his for honest work.

YOU MUST NOT LIE. / When we lie to each other we are hurting ourselves.

YOU MUST NOT BE ENVIOUS. / Wherever there is jealousy...there will be disorder and every other kind of evil.

The whole Law can be summed up in this one command: Love others as you love yourself.

Exodus 20:13. Matthew 5:22. Exodus 20:14.
1 Thessalonians 4:7. Exodus 20:15. Ephesians 4:28.
Exodus 20:16. Ephesians 4:25. Exodus 20:17.
James 3:16. Galatians 5:14.

EXODUS

Who is Jehovah?

He is my God, and I will praise him.
He is my father's God—I will exalt him.
The Lord is a warrior—
Yes, Jehovah is his name.

He is your helper; he is your shield. He is a father to the fatherless; he gives justice to the widows, for he is holy. He gives families to the lonely, and releases prisoners from jail, singing with joy!

Jehovah God is our Light and our Protector. He gives us grace and glory. No good thing will he withhold from those who walk along his paths.

What a glorious Lord! He who daily bears our burdens also gives us our salvation.

Sing praises to the Lord, to him who rides upon the ancient heavens, whose mighty voice thunders from the sky.

Exodus 5:2. Exodus 15:2,3. Psalm 115:11. Psalm 68:5,6. Psalm 84:11. Psalm 68:19,32,33.

You must therefore be holy, for I am holy.

You shall be holy to me, for I the Lord am holy, and I have set you apart from all other peoples, to be mine. Obey me and live as you should. He gave you his rules for daily life so you would know what he wanted you to do.

Happy are all who perfectly follow the laws of God. Happy are all who search for God and always do his will, rejecting compromise with evil, and walking only in his paths.

Fix your thoughts on what is true and good and right. Think about things that are pure and lovely, and dwell on the fine, good things in others.

Truth rises from the earth and righteousness smiles down from heaven. Stand before the Lord in awe.

Leviticus 11:45. Leviticus 20:26. Genesis 17:1. Romans 9:4. Psalm 119:1-3. Philippians 4:8. Psalm 85:11. Psalm 4:4.

LEVITICUS

Worship the Lord with the beauty of holy lives.

The Lord had made a contract...they were never to worship or make sacrifices to any heathen gods. They were to worship only the Lord who had brought them out of the land of Egypt with such tremendous miracles and power.

"Call them all together," the Lord instructed, "men, women, children, and foreigners living among you to hear the laws of God and to learn his will."

Give him the glory he deserves! Bring your offering and come to worship him.

Let the heavens be glad, the earth rejoice. Let the vastness of the roaring seas demonstrate his glory.

Psalm 96:9. 2 Kings 17:35,36. Deuteronomy 31:12.
Psalm 96:8,11.

LEVITICUS

**I will show myself
holy among those
who approach me,
and I will be
glorified before
all the people.**

Who else is like the Lord
Among the gods?
Who is glorious in holiness like him?
Who is so awesome in splendor,
A wonder-working God?

Great and marvelous
Are your doings,
Lord God Almighty.
Just and true
Are your ways,
O King of Ages.
Who shall not fear,
O Lord,
And glorify your Name?
For you alone are holy.

Leviticus 10:3. Exodus 15:11. Revelation
15:3,4.

**You must respect your mothers
and fathers and obey my Sabbath law,
for I am the Lord your God.**

Obedience is far better than sacrifice. He is much more interested in your listening to him than in your offering the fat of rams to him. For rebellion is as bad as the sin of witchcraft, and stubbornness is as bad as worshiping idols.

Only fools refuse to be taught. Listen to your father and mother. What you learn from them will stand you in good stead. It will gain you many honors.

Follow only what is good. Remember that those who do what is right prove that they are God's children, and those who continue in evil prove that they are far from God.

Leviticus 19:2. 1 Samuel 15:22,23.
Proverbs 1:8,9. 3 John 11.

LEVITICUS

Don't seek vengeance.
Don't bear a grudge.

They are always twisting what I say.
They repay me evil for good and
hate me for standing for the right.
When that happens, rejoice! Yes,
leap for joy! For you will have a
great reward awaiting you in
heaven. And you will be in good
company—the ancient prophets
were treated that way too!
Love your enemies. Do good to
those who hate you. Pray for the
happiness of those who curse you.
Implore God's blessing on those
who hurt you.
All that happens to us is working
for our good if we love God and are
fitting into his plans.
I, even I, (God) am he who
comforts you and gives you all this
joy.

Leviticus 19:18. Psalm 56:5. Psalm 38:20.
Luke 6:23,27,28. Romans 8:28. Isaiah 51:12.

If you have extra food, give it away to those who are hungry.

When you harvest your crops, don't reap the corners of your fields, and don't pick up the stray grains of wheat from the ground. It is the same with your grape crop—don't strip every last piece of fruit from the vines, and don't pick up the grapes that fall to the ground. Leave them for the poor and for those traveling through, for I am Jehovah your God.

   If you are really eager to give, then it isn't important how much you have to give. God wants you to give what you have, not what you haven't. This is one way to prove that your love is real, that it goes beyond mere words.

Luke 3:11. Leviticus 19:9,10. 2 Corinthians 8:12,8.

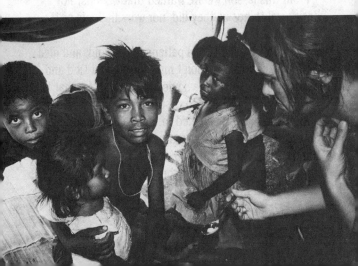

NUMBERS

You may be sure that your sin will catch up with you.

We must never forget...what has happened to our people in the wilderness long ago.

From this lesson we are warned that we must not desire evil things as they did, nor worship idols as they did.

And don't try the Lord's patience—they did, and died from snake bites. And don't murmur against God and his dealings with you, as some of them did, for that is why God sent his Angel to destroy them.

All these things happened to them as examples—as object lessons to us—to warn us against doing the same things. They were written down so that we could read about them and learn from them in these last days as the world nears its end.

Numbers 32:23. 1 Corinthians 10:1,6,7,9-11.

**Jehovah now instructed Moses,
"Send spies into the land of Canaan."**

Forty days later they returned from their tour. This was
their report: "We arrived in the land you sent us to see,
and it is indeed a magnificent country...But the people
living there are powerful, and their cities are fortified
and very large."

But Caleb reassured the people as they stood before
Moses. "Let us go up at once and possess it," he said,
"for we are well able to conquer it!"

"Not against people as strong as they are!" the other
spies said. "They would crush us!" So the majority
report was negative.

God says, "I was very angry with them, for their hearts
were always looking somewhere else instead of up to
me, and they never found the paths I wanted them to
follow."

You can never please God without faith, without
depending on him.

Numbers 13:1,2,25,27,28,30-32. Hebrews 3:10. Hebrews 11:6.

NUMBERS

Anything is possible if you have faith.

But my servant Caleb is a different kind of man—he has obeyed me fully. I will bring him into the land he entered as a spy, and his descendants shall have their full share in it.

The Lord has kept me (Caleb) alive and well for all these forty-five years since crisscrossing the wilderness, and today I am 85 years old. I am as strong now as I was when Moses sent us on that journey, and I can still travel and fight as well as I could then!

It is better to trust the Lord than to put confidence in men. It is better to take refuge in him than in the mightiest king!

Mark 9:23. Numbers 14:24,10. Psalm 118:8,9.

Jehovah has sent me (Moses) to do all these things that I have done— for I have not done them on my own.

Miriam and Aaron . . . said, "Has the Lord spoken only through Moses? Hasn't he spoken through us, too?"

The Lord heard them. Immediately he summoned Moses, Aaron and Miriam to the Tabernacle . . . And the Lord said to them . . . "With him (Moses) I speak face to face! And he shall see the very form of God! Why then were you not afraid to criticize him?"

Miriam suddenly became white with leprosy. When Aaron saw what had happened, he cried out to Moses, "Oh, sir, do not punish us for this sin. We were fools to do such a thing."

Obey your spiritual leaders and be willing to do what they say. Honor the officers of your church who work hard among you and warn you against all that is wrong. Think highly of them and give them your wholehearted love.

Numbers 16:28. Numbers 12:1-3,6,8,10,11. Hebrews 13:17.
1 Thessalonians 5:12,13.

NUMBERS

The manna
fell with the dew
during the night.

The manna was about the size of coriander seed, and looked like droplets of gum from the bark of a tree. The people...made pancakes from it.

The people were soon complaining. "Oh, for a few bites of meat! Oh, that we had some of the delicious fish we enjoyed so much in Egypt, and the wonderful cucumbers and melons, leeks, onions and garlic!"

Be satisfied with what you have. For everything God made is good, and we may eat it gladly if you are thankful for it. Food isn't everything...real life comes by obeying every command of God.

Numbers 11:9,7,8,1,4,5. Hebrews 13:5.
1 Timothy 4:4. Deuteronomy 8:3.

The people were very discouraged.

They began to murmur against God and to complain against Moses. "There is nothing to eat here, and nothing to drink, and we hate this insipid manna."

So the Lord sent poisonous snakes among them to punish them, and many of them were bitten and died. Then the people came to Moses and cried out, "We have sinned, for we have spoken against Jehovah and against you. Pray to him to take away the snakes."

Then the Lord told him, "Make a bronze replica of one of these snakes and attach it to the top of a pole; anyone who is bitten shall live if he simply looks at it."

I, the Messiah, have come to earth, and will return to heaven again. And as Moses lifted up the bronze image of a serpent on a pole, even so I must be lifted up upon a pole, so that everyone who believes in me will have eternal life.

Numbers 21:4-8. John 3:13-15.

NUMBERS

The rich and poor are alike before the Lord who made them all. There is the same law for all, native-born or foreigner, and this shall be true forever from generation to generation.

He doesn't care how great a man may be and he doesn't pay more attention to the rich than to the poor.

You have no right to criticize your brother or look down on him. Remember, each of us will stand personally before the Judgment Seat of God.

One's nationality or race or education or social position is unimportant. Such things mean nothing. Whether a person has Christ is what matters, and he is equally available to all.

Numbers 15:16.
Proverbs 22:2.
Numbers 15:15,16.
Job 34:19.
Romans 14:10.
Colossians 3:11.

**All are
equal
before
the Lord.**

Moses...said all these things to the people of Israel.

The Lord your God has watched over you and blessed you every step of the way for all these forty years as you have wandered around in this great wilderness and you have lacked nothing in all that time.

I am giving you the choice today between God's blessing or God's curse! There will be blessing if you obey the commandments of the Lord your God...and a curse if you refuse them.

These laws are not mere words—they are your life! Through obeying them you will live long, plentiful lives.

Choose to love the Lord your God and to obey him and to cling to him, for he is your life and the length of your days. Deuteronomy 31:1; 2:7; 11:26-28; 32:47; 30:20.

DEUTERONOMY

The eternal God is your Refuge, and underneath are the everlasting arms.

He thrusts out your enemies before you; it is he who cries, "Destroy them!"

Blessed is the man who trusts in the Lord and has made the Lord his hope and confidence. He is like a tree planted along a riverbank, with its roots reaching deep into the water—a tree not bothered by the heat nor worried by long months of drought. Its leaves stay green and it goes right on producing all its luscious fruit.

I will be your God through all your lifetime, yes, even when your hair is white with age. I made you and I will care for you. I will carry you along and be your Savior.

Deuteronomy 33:27. Jeremiah 17:7. Isaiah 46:4.

DEUTERONOMY

**Listen carefully now to all
these laws God has given you.
Learn them, and be sure to obey them!**
If you obey them they will give you a reputation for
wisdom and intelligence. Tie them on your finger, wear
them on your forehead, and write them on the doorposts
of your house!

But watch out! Be very careful never to forget what
you have seen God doing for you. May his miracles have
a deep and permanent effect upon your lives! Write them
deep within your heart.

If you want favor with both God and man, and a
reputation for good judgment and common sense, then
trust the Lord completely.

Deuteronomy 5:1. Deuteronomy 4:6. Deuteronomy 6:8,9. Deuteronomy 4:9.
Proverbs 3:3,4,5.

Obeying these commandments is not something beyond your strength and reach.

For these laws are not in the far heavens, so distant that you can't hear and obey them, and with no one to bring them down to you. Nor are they beyond the ocean, so far that no one can bring you their message. But they are very close at hand—in your hearts and on your lips—so obey them.

You have every grace and blessing. Every spiritual gift and power for doing his will are yours during this time of waiting for the return of our Lord Jesus Christ.

Deuteronomy 30:11-14. 1 Corinthians 1:7.

DEUTERONOMY

What does the Lord your God require of you?

1. To listen carefully to all he says to you, and
2. To obey for your own good the commandments I am giving you today, and
3. To love him and to worship him with all your hearts and souls.

If a person just listens and doesn't obey, he is like a man looking at his face in a mirror; as soon as he walks away, he can't see himself anymore or remember what he looks like. But if anyone keeps looking steadily into God's law for free men, he will not only remember it but he will do what it says, and God will greatly bless him in everything he does.

Loving God means doing what he tells us to do, and really, that isn't hard at all. For every child of God can obey him ... by trusting Christ to help him.

Deuteronomy 10:12,13.
James 1:23-25. 1 John 5:3,4.

For it always goes well with us when we obey all the laws of the Lord our God.

Jehovah is our God, Jehovah alone. You must love him with all your heart, soul, and might. And you must think constantly about these commandments.

One of the teachers of religion . . . asked, "Of all the commandments which is the most important?"

Jesus replied, "The one that says, 'Hear O Israel! The Lord our God is the one and only God. And you must love him with all your heart and soul and mind and strength.'

"The second is, 'You must love others as much as yourself.' No other commandments are greater than these."

Deuteronomy 6:25,4-6. Mark 12:28-33.

DEUTERONOMY

There has never been another prophet like Moses.

Moses was born—a child of divine beauty. He became a mighty prince and orator.

Moses . . . chose to share ill-treatment with God's people instead of enjoying the fleeting pleasures of sin.

In the wilderness Moses was the go-between—the mediator between the people of Israel and the Angel who gave them the Law of God—the Living Word—on Mount Sinai.

By means of many remarkable miracles he led them out of Egypt and through the Red Sea, and back and forth through the wilderness for forty years.

Moses was 120 years old when he died, yet his eyesight was perfect and he was as strong as a young man.

Deuteronomy 34:10. Acts 7:20,22. Hebrews 11:24,25. Acts 7:38,36. Deuteronomy 34:7.

Michelangelo, *Moses*, Vatican, Alinari/Art Resource

DEUTERONOMY

Bring all the tithes into the storehouse.

The purpose of tithing is to teach you always to put God first in your lives. Cheerful givers are the ones God prizes.

God is able to make it up to you by giving you everything you need and more, so that there will not only be enough for your own needs, but plenty left over to give joyfully to others.

God will give you much so that you can give away much.

Blessed Lord, teach me your rules. I have recited your laws, and rejoiced in them more than in riches. I will meditate upon them and give them my full respect. I will delight in them and not forget them.

Malachi 3:10. Deuteronomy 14:23.
2 Corinthians 9:7,8,11. Psalm
119:12-16.

JOSHUA

Don't ever be afraid or discouraged.

God spoke to ... Joshua and said to him ... "Lead my people across the Jordan River into the Promised Land.

"I will not abandon you or fail to help you. You need only to be strong and courageous and to obey to the letter every law Moses gave you, for if you are careful to obey every one of them you will be successful in everything you do. Be bold and strong! Banish fear and doubt! For remember, the Lord your God is with you wherever you go."

Oh, the joys of those who do not follow evil men's advice, who do not hang around with sinners, scoffing at the things of God. But they delight in doing everything God wants them to, and day and night are always meditating on his laws and thinking about ways to follow him more closely.

Joshua 10:25. Joshua 1:1,2,5,7,9. Psalm 1:1,2.

JOSHUA

Tomorrow, the Lord will do a great miracle.

Joshua and all the people of Israel . . . arrived . . . at the banks of the Jordan River.

It was the harvest season and the Jordan was overflowing all its banks. But as the people set out to cross the river . . . the water began piling up as though against a dam! And the water below that point flowed on to the Dead Sea until the riverbed was empty. Then all the people crossed at a spot where the river was close to the city of Jericho.

How awe-inspiring are your deeds, O God! How great your power! No wonder your enemies surrender! All the earth shall worship you and sing of your glories.

Joshua 3:5,1,13-16. Psalm 66:3,4.

JOSHUA

It was faith that brought the walls of Jericho tumbling down.

The Lord said to Joshua, "Jericho and its king and all its mighty warriors are already defeated, for I have given them to you! Your entire army is to walk around the city once a day for six days, followed by seven priests walking ahead of the Ark, each carrying a trumpet made from a ram's horn. On the seventh day you are to walk around the city seven times, with all the priests blowing their trumpets. Then, when they give a long, loud blast, all the people are to give a mighty shout and the walls of the city will fall down. Then move in upon the city from every direction."

This so-called "foolish" plan of God is far wiser than the wisest plan of the wisest man. God has deliberately chosen to use ideas the world considers foolish and of little worth ... so that no one anywhere can ever brag in the presence of God.

Hebrews 11:30. Joshua 6:2-5. 1 Corinthians 1:25,27,29.

There was sin among the Israelis. They were soundly defeated.

The Lord said to Joshua, "Israel has sinned and disobeyed my commandment and has taken loot when I said it was not to be taken. They have not only taken it, they have lied about it and have hidden it among their belongings."

Joshua said to Achan, "Make your confession. Tell me what you have done."

Achan replied, "I saw a beautiful robe imported from Babylon, and some silver worth $200, and a bar of gold worth $500. I wanted them so much that I took them."

Would God not know it? Yes, he knows the secrets of every heart.

O God, you know so well how stupid I am, and you know all my sins. Don't let me be a stumbling block to those who trust in you.

Joshua 7:1,4,10,11,19-21.
Psalm 44:21. Psalm 69:5,6.

JOSHUA

**Use every piece of God's armor
to resist the enemy whenever he attacks,
and when it is all over,
you will still be standing up.**

Take your share of suffering as a good soldier of Jesus Christ . . . and as Christ's soldier do not let yourself become tied up in worldly affairs, for then you cannot satisfy the one who enlisted you in his army.

Here on earth you will have many trials and sorrows. But cheer up, for I have overcome the world.

Joshua took the entire land just as the Lord had instructed Moses. And he gave it to the people of Israel as their inheritance, dividing the land among the tribes. So the land finally rested from its war.

Ephesians 6:13. 2 Timothy 2:3,4. John 16:33. Joshua 11:23.

JOSHUA

**The decision as to
which tribe would receive
which area was decided
by throwing dice
before the Lord,
and he caused them
to turn up
in the ways he wanted.**

The Lord said, "My servant Caleb is a different kind of man—he has obeyed me fully. I will bring him into the land he entered as a spy, and his descendants shall have their full share in it."

Joshua blessed him (Caleb) and gave him Hebron as a permanent inheritance because he had followed the Lord God of Israel.

The Most High dominates the kingdoms of the world, and gives them to anyone he wants to, even the lowliest of men!

Oh, put God to the test and see how kind he is! See for yourself the way his mercies shower down on all who trust in him.

Joshua 14:1,2. Numbers 14:24. Joshua 14:13,14.
Daniel 4:17. Psalm 34:8.

JOSHUA

We choose the Lord, for he alone is our God.

Joshua made a covenant with them that day at Shechem, committing them to a permanent and binding contract between themselves and God.

If you tell others with your own mouth that Jesus Christ is your Lord, and believe in your own heart that God has raised him from the dead, you will be saved. For it is by believing in his heart that a man becomes right with God; and with his mouth he tells others of his faith, confirming his salvation.

The Scriptures tell us that no one who believes in Christ will ever be disappointed.

Joshua 24:18,25. Romans 10:9-11.

JUDGES

Every man did whatever he thought was right.

They did many things which the Lord had expressly forbidden, including the worshiping of heathen gods. They abandoned Jehovah. So the anger of the Lord flamed out against all Israel. He left them to the mercy of their enemies.

They kept on doing whatever they wanted to, following their own stubborn, evil thoughts. They went backward instead of forward.

Beware then of your own hearts ... lest you find that they, too, are evil and unbelieving and are leading you away from the Living God.

Judges 21:25. Judges 2:11-14. Jeremiah 7:24. Hebrews 3:12.

JUDGES

Praise the Lord!
Israel's leaders bravely led;
The people gladly followed!
Yes, bless the Lord!

Israel's leader . . . the one who was responsible for bringing the people back to God, was Deborah, a prophetess.

One day she summoned Barak, and said to him, "The Lord God of Israel has commanded you to mobilize ten thousand men. Lead them to Mount Tabor, to fight King Jabin's mighty army with all his chariots. The Lord says, 'I will

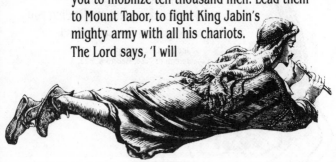

draw them to the Kishon River, and you will
defeat them there.' "
　　It would take too long to recount the stories
of the faith of Gideon and Barak and Samson
. . . and all the other prophets. These people all
trusted God and as a result won battles,
overthrew kingdoms, ruled their people well,
and received what God had promised them.

The village musicians
Gather at the village well
To sing of the triumphs of the Lord.
Judges 5:2. Judges 4:4, 6, 7. Hebrews 11:32, 33. Judges 5:11.

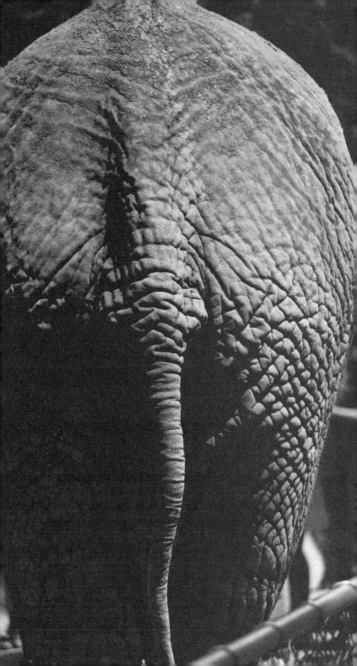

JUDGES

God wants us to turn from godless living and sinful pleasures.

When the nation of Israel went out to battle against its enemies, the Lord blocked their path. He had warned them about this. But when the people were in this terrible plight, the Lord raised up judges to save them from their enemies.

Each judge rescued the people of Israel from their enemies throughout his lifetime, for the Lord was moved to pity by the groaning of his people under their crushing oppressions. So he helped them as long as that judge lived. But when the judge died, the people turned from doing right and behaved even worse than their ancestors had.

Don't be misled; remember that you can't ignore God and get away with it: a man will always reap just the kind of crop he sows!

Titus 2:12. Judges 2:15, 16, 18, 19. Galatians 6:7.

JUDGES

The wisest of men who worship idols are altogether stupid and foolish.

The people of Israel began once again to worship other gods, and once again the Lord let their enemies harass them. The Midianites were so cruel that the Israelites took to the mountains, living in caves and dens. Israel was reduced to abject poverty because of the Midianites.

Who are these who sit in darkness, in the shadow of death, crushed by misery and slavery? They rebelled against the Lord, scorning him who is the God above all gods. That is why he broke them with hard labor. Then they cried to the Lord in their troubles, and he rescued them! He was grieved by their misery.

Oh, that my people would listen to me! Oh, that Israel would follow me, walking in my paths!

Jeremiah 10:8. Judges 6:1, 2, 6. Psalm 107:10. Judges 10:16. Psalm 81:13.

JUDGES

Apart from me you can't do a thing.

Gideon ... was hiding from the Midianites.

The Lord turned to him and said, "I will make you strong! Go and save Israel from the Midianites! I am sending you!"

But Gideon replied, "Sir, how can I save Israel? My family is the poorest in the whole tribe of Manasseh, and I am the least thought of in the entire family!"

Whereupon the Lord said to him, "But I, Jehovah, will be with you!"

That is all you need. My power shows up best in weak people. Few of you who follow Christ have big names or power or wealth.

John 15:5. Judges 6:11, 14-16. 2 Corinthians 12:9. 1 Corinthians 1:26.

JUDGES

Guard well the splendid, God-given ability you received as a gift from the Holy Spirit who lives within you.

A young lion attacked Samson in the vineyards on the outskirts of the town. At that moment the Spirit of the Lord came mightily upon him and since he had no weapon, he ripped the lion's jaws apart, and did it as easily as though it were a young goat!

The God of Israel gives strength and mighty power to his people. Blessed be God!

Riches and honor come from you alone, and you are the Ruler of all mankind. Your hand controls power and might, and it is at your discretion that men are made great and given strength. Everything we have has come from you, and we only give you what is yours already!

Fight on for God. Hold tightly to the eternal life which God has given you.

2 Timothy 1:14.

Judges 14:5, 6. Psalm 68:35.

1 Chronicles 29:12, 14.

1 Timothy 6:12.

JUDGES

A city or home divided against itself cannot stand.

(Samson) finally told her (Delilah) his secret.

"If my hair were cut, my strength would leave me, and I would become as weak as anyone else." . . . They cut off his hair. Then she screamed, "The Philistines are here to capture you, Samson!" So the Philistines captured him and gouged out his eyes.

Above all else, guard your affections. For they influence everything else in your life. Watch yourself, lest you be indiscreet and betray some vital information.

No wonder you are in darkness when you expected light. No wonder you are walking in the gloom. No wonder you grope like blind men and stumble along in broad daylight.

Watch your step . . . and don't associate with radicals.

Matthew 12:25. Judges 16:16, 17, 19-21.
Proverbs 4:23. Proverbs 5:2. Isaiah 59:9, 10.
Proverbs 24:21.

RUTH

**If you give, you will get!
Your gift will return to you
in full and overflowing measure.**

Boaz went over and talked to her (Ruth). "Stay right here with us to glean."

She thanked him warmly. "How can you be so kind to me?" she asked. "You must know I am only a foreigner."

"Yes, I know," Boaz replied, "and I also know about all the love and kindness you have shown your mother-in-law since the death of your husband, and how you left your father and mother in your own land and have come here to live among strangers. May the Lord God of Israel, under whose wings you have come to take refuge, bless you for it."

So she sat with his reapers and he gave her food, more than she could eat.

Luke 6:38. Ruth 2:8-12, 14.

Historical Books

1 & 2 SAMUEL, 1 & 2 KINGS, 1 & 2 CHRONICLES

Who is this King of Glory? The Lord, strong and mighty, invincible in battle.

The Lord declares, "This is the King of my choice, and I have enthroned him in Jerusalem, my holy city."

You gave me victory in every battle. The nations came and served me. Even those I didn't know before come now and bow before me. Foreigners who have never seen me submit instantly.

Arm yourself, O Mighty One, so glorious, so majestic! And in your majesty go on to victory, defending truth, humility, and justice. Go forth to awe-inspiring deeds! Your arrows are sharp in your enemies' hearts; they fall before you. Your throne, O God, endures forever. Justice is your royal scepter. You love what is good and hate what is wrong. Therefore God, your God, has given you more gladness than anyone else.

Psalm 24:8. Psalm 2:6.
Psalm 18:43, 44. Psalm 45:3-7.

The Lord your God was already your King, for he has always been your King.

King of Kings, and Lord of Lords. All will bow before him! All will serve him!

Jesus said, "I was born for that purpose. And I came to bring truth to the world."

The leaders of Israel met. . .with Samuel.

"Give us a king like all the other nations have," they pleaded.

"Do as they say," the Lord replied, "for I am the one they are rejecting. But warn them about what it will be like to have a king!"

So Samuel told the people what the Lord had said: . . . "You will shed bitter tears because of this king you are demanding."

"Even so, we still want a king," they said, "for we want to be like the nations around us."

1 Samuel 12:12. Revelation 19:16.
Psalm 72:11. John 18:37.
1 Samuel 8:4, 5, 7, 9, 10, 18-20.

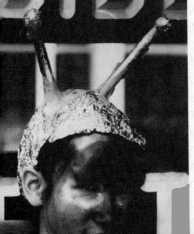

Historical Books

Where is he? Is he here among us?

Kish was a rich, influential man from the tribe of Benjamin. His son Saul was the most handsome man in Israel. And he was head and shoulders taller than anyone else in the land!

When Samuel saw Saul the Lord said, "That's the man I told you about! He will rule my people."

Then Samuel took a flask of olive oil and poured it over Saul's head and kissed him on the cheek and said, "I am doing this because the Lord has appointed you to be the king of his people, Israel!

"At that time the Spirit of the Lord will come mightily upon you, and you will prophesy with them and you will feel and act like a different person. From that time on your decisions should be based on whatever seems best under the circumstances, for the Lord will guide you."

The Most High God . . . gives power to anyone he chooses.

1 Samuel 10:22. 1 Samuel 9:1, 2, 17. 1 Samuel 10:1, 6, 7. Daniel 4:25.

If you won't listen to the Lord your God . . . you will be confused and a failure in everything you do.

Samuel said to Saul, "Here is (God's) commandment to you: . . . 'Completely destroy the entire Amalek nation.'"

Saul and his men kept the best of the sheep and oxen and the fattest of the lambs—everything, in fact, that appealed to them. They destroyed only what was worthless or of poor quality.

Samuel replied (to Saul) . . . "Obedience is far better than sacrifice. He (God) is much more interested in your listening to him than in your offering the fat of rams to him. For rebellion is as bad as the sin of witchcraft, and stubbornness is as bad as worshiping idols. And now because you have rejected the word of Jehovah, he has rejected you from being king." For the Lord wants a man who will obey him.

And the Lord was sorry that he had ever made Saul king of Israel.

Deuteronomy 28:15, 20. 1 Samuel 15:1-3, 9, 22, 23. 1 Samuel 13:14. 1 Samuel 15:35.

Historical Books

Goliath the giant . . . insulted the entire army of Israel.

"Don't worry about a thing," David told (King Saul). "I'll take care of this Philistine!

"The Lord who saved me from the claws and teeth of the lion and the bear will save me from this Philistine!"

Goliath walked out toward David . . . sneering in contempt at this nice little red-cheeked boy!

David shouted in reply, " . . . I come to you in the name of the Lord . . . the whole world will know that there is a God in Israel! And Israel will learn that the Lord does not depend on weapons to fulfill his plans—he works without regard to human means! He will give you to us!"

So David conquered the Philistine giant with a sling and a stone.

1 Samuel 17:23, 25, 32, 37, 41, 42, 45-47, 50.

Historical Books

Jealousy is more dangerous and cruel than anger.

After David had killed Goliath . . . Saul was very angry. "They credit David with ten thousands and me with only thousands. Next they'll be making him their king!"

So from that time on King Saul kept a jealous watch on David. The very next day, in fact, . . . Saul, who was fiddling with his spear, suddenly hurled it at David intending to pin him to the wall.

Saul was afraid of him and jealous because the Lord had left him and was now with David.

Wherever there is jealousy or selfish ambition, there will be disorder and every other kind of evil. Every kind of wickedness and sin, of greed and hate, envy, murder, fighting, lying, bitterness, and gossip.

Proverbs 27:4. 1 Samuel 18:6, 8, 9-12. James 3:16. Romans 1:29.

Lord, waken!
See what's happening!

When the king realized how much the Lord was with David and how immensely popular he was with all the people, he became even more afraid of him, and grew to hate him more with every passing day.

Saul sent troops to watch David's house and kill him when he came out in the morning.

David speaks: "O my God, save me from my enemies. Protect me from these who have come to destroy me. Preserve me from these criminals, these murderers. They lurk in ambush for my life. Strong men are out there waiting. And not, O Lord, because I've done them wrong. Yet they prepare to kill me.

O God my Strength! I will sing your praises, for you are my place of safety. My God is changeless in his love for me and he will come and help me. You have been my high tower of refuge, a place of safety in the day of my distress."

Psalm 59:4. 1 Samuel 18:28, 29. 1 Samuel 19:11. Psalm 59:1-4, 9, 10, 16.

Historical Books

Saul was dead.

The Philistines closed in on Saul, and killed his sons Jonathan, Abinidab, and Malchishua. Then the archers overtook Saul and wounded him badly. . . . So Saul took his own sword and fell upon the point of the blade, and it pierced him through.

When the people of Jabesh-gilead heard what the Philistines had done to Saul, their heroic warriors went out to the battlefield and brought back his body and the bodies of his three sons. Then they buried them beneath the oak tree at Jabesh and mourned and fasted for seven days.

Saul died for his disobedience to the Lord and because he had consulted a medium, and did not ask the Lord for guidance. So the Lord killed him and gave the kingdom to David, the son of Jesse.

2 Samuel 1:1. 1 Samuel 31:2-4. 1 Chronicles 10:11-14.

**Do not rejoice
when your enemy meets trouble.
Let there be no gladness when he falls.**

David and his men ... mourned and wept and fasted all day for Saul and his son Jonathan ... who had died that day.

   Then David composed a dirge (funeral song) for Saul and Jonathan ...

O Mount Gilboa,
Let there be no dew nor rain upon you,
Let no crops of grain grow on your slopes.
For there the mighty Saul has died;
He is God's appointed king no more.

Be gentle and ready to forgive. Never hold grudges. Remember, the Lord forgave you, so you must forgive others.

Proverbs 24:17. 2 Samuel 1:11, 12, 17, 21. Colossians 3:13.

Historical Books

**The leaders of Judah
came to David
and crowned him king.
Then representatives of
all the tribes of Israel
crowned him king of Israel.**

The Lord has said that you should be the shepherd and leader of his people.

He chose his servant David, taking him from feeding sheep, and from following the ewes with lambs. God presented David to his people, as their shepherd and he cared for them with a true heart and skillful hands.

And David became more and more famous and powerful, for the Lord of the heavens was with him.

Come before him with thankful hearts. Let us sing him psalms of praise. For the Lord is a great God, the great King of all gods.

Come, kneel before the Lord our Maker, for he is our God. We are his sheep and he is our Shepherd.

2 Samuel 2:4. 2 Samuel 5:1, 3, 2. Psalm 78:70-72.
1 Chronicles 11:9. Psalm 95:2, 3, 6, 7.

He, the Holy One of Israel, has given us our king.

He is my servant David! I have anointed him with my holy oil. I will steady him and make him strong. His enemies shall not outwit him, nor shall the wicked overpower him. I will beat down his adversaries before him, and destroy those who hate him. I will protect and bless him constantly and surround him with my love. He will be great because of me.

I will treat him as my firstborn son, and make him the mightiest king in all the earth. I will love him forever, and be kind to him always. My covenant with him will never end.

Psalm 89:18, 20-24, 27, 28.

Historical Books

David became greater and greater for the Lord God of heaven was with him.

In my distress I prayed to the Lord and he answered me and rescued me. He is for me! How can I be afraid? What can mere man do to me? The Lord is on my side. He will help me. Let those who hate me beware.

It is better to trust the Lord than to put confidence in men. It is better to take refuge in him than in the mightiest king! Though all the nations of the world attack me, I will march out behind his banner and destroy them.

He is my strength and song in the heat of battle, and now he has given me the victory.

You are my God, and I shall give you this thanks and this praise.

2 Samuel 5:10. Psalm 118:5-10, 14, 28.

**I will sing
about your
lovingkindness
and your justice,
Lord.
I will sing
your praises!**

David now realized why the Lord had made him king and why he had made his kingdom so great. It was for a special reason—to give joy to God's people!

I will try to walk a blameless path, but how I need your help, especially in my own home, where I long to act as I should.

Help me to refuse the low and vulgar things. Help me to abhor all crooked deals of every kind, to have no part in them. I will reject all selfishness and stay away from every evil.

I will make the godly of the land my heroes, and invite them to my home. Only those who are truly good shall be my servants.

Psalm 101:1. 1 Chronicles 14:2. Psalm 101:2-4, 6.

Historical Books

David did as the Lord commanded him.

He cut down the army of the Philistines all the way from Gibeon to Gezer. David's fame spread everywhere, and the Lord caused all the nations to fear him.

Lord, with all my heart I thank you. I will sing your praises before the armies of angels in heaven. I face your Temple as I worship, giving thanks to you for all your lovingkindness and your faithfulness, for your promises are backed by all the honor of your name. When I pray, you answer me, and encourage me by giving me the strength I need.

Though I am surrounded by troubles, you will bring me safely through them. You will clench your fist against my angry enemies! Your power will save me. The Lord will work out his plans for my life—for your lovingkindness, Lord, continues forever.

1 Chronicles 14:16, 17. Psalm 138:1-3, 7, 8.

Ascribe to the Lord
The glory due his name!

David began the custom of using choirs in the
Tabernacle to sing thanksgiving to the Lord.

Oh, give thanks to the Lord and
  pray to him, they sang.
Tell the peoples of the world
About his mighty doings.
Sing to him; yes, sing his praises
And tell of his marvelous works.
Glory in his holy name;
Let all rejoice who seek the Lord.
Seek the Lord; yes, seek his strength
And seek his face untiringly.
Sing to the Lord, O earth,
Declare each day that he is
  the one who saves!
Show his glory to the
  nations!
Tell everyone about his
  miracles.
For the Lord is great,
  and should be
  highly praised.

1 Chronicles 16:29,
7-11, 23-25.

Historical Books

O loving
and kind God,
have mercy.

The Lord God of Israel says, "I made you king of Israel
and saved you from the power of Saul. I gave you his
palace and his wives and the kingdoms of Israel and
Judah. And if that had not been enough, I would have
given you much, much more. Why, then, have you
despised the laws of God and done this horrible deed?
For you have murdered Uriah and stolen his wife."

David speaks:
"I admit my shameful deed—it haunts
me day and night. It is against you and you alone I
sinned, and did this terrible thing. You saw it all, and
your sentence against me is just.

  "After you have punished me, give me back my joy
again. Don't keep looking at my sins—erase them from
your sight. Create in me a new, clean heart, O God, filled
with clean thoughts and right desires."

Psalm 51:1. 2 Samuel 12:7-9. Psalm 51:3, 4, 8-10.

Historical Books

What happiness for those whose guilt has been forgiven!

What joys when sins are covered over! What relief for those who have confessed their sins and God has cleared their record.

There was a time when I wouldn't admit what a sinner I was. But my dishonesty made me miserable and filled my days with frustration. All day and all night your hand was heavy on me. My strength evaporated like water on a sunny day until I finally admitted all my sins to you and stopped trying to hide them. I said to myself, "I will confess them to the Lord." And you forgave me! All my guilt is gone.

Now I say that each believer should confess his sins to God when he is aware of them, while there is time to be forgiven. Judgment will not touch him if he does.

Psalm 32:1-6.

Historical Books

May this bring eternal honor to your name

After David had been living in his new palace for some time he said to Nathan the prophet, "Look, I'm living here in a cedar-paneled home while the Ark of the Covenant of God is out there in a tent!"

That same night God said to Nathan, "Go and give my servant David this message: 'You are not to build my temple!'

" 'When your time here on earth is over and you die, I will place one of your sons upon your throne. He is the one who shall build me a temple.' "

David ordered all the leaders of Israel to assist his son in this project. "Try with every fiber of your being to obey the Lord your God, and you will soon be bringing the Ark and the other holy articles of worship into the Temple of the Lord!"

1 Chronicles 17:24, 1, 3, 4, 11, 12. 1 Chronicles 22:17, 19.

Courtesy of **LEGO** Systems, Inc.

Historical Books

King David went in and sat before the Lord.

Who am I, O Lord God, and what is my family, that you have given me all this? For all the great things you have already done for me are nothing in comparison to what you have promised to do in the future!

O Lord, you have given me these wonderful promises just because you want to be kind to me, because of your own great heart. O Lord, there is no one like you—there is no other God. In fact, we have never even heard of another god like you!

The Lord himself is my inheritance, my prize. He is my food and drink, my highest joy! He guards all that is mine.

I will bless the Lord who counsels me. He gives me wisdom in the night. He tells me what to do.

1 Chronicles 17:16, 17, 19, 20. Psalm 16:5, 7.

Historical Books

King David has declared Solomon as king!

As the time of King David's death approached, he gave this charge to his son Solomon:

"I am going where every man on earth must some day go. I am counting on you to be a strong and worthy successor. Obey the laws of God and follow all his ways. Keep each of his commands written in the law of Moses so that you will prosper in everything you do, wherever you turn.

"So now, my son, may the Lord be with you and prosper you as you do what he told you to do and build the Temple of the Lord. And may the Lord give you the good judgment to follow all his laws when he makes you king of Israel."

And Solomon became the new king . . . and his kingdom prospered.

1 Kings 1:43. 1 Kings 2:1-3. 1 Chronicles 22:11, 12. 1 Kings 2:12.

**O Lord my God . . .
I (Solomon) am as
a little child
who doesn't know
his way around.**

Give me an understanding mind so that I can govern
your people well and know the difference between what
is right and what is wrong. For who by himself is able to
carry such a heavy responsibility?

I, Wisdom, give good advice and common sense.
Because of my strength, kings reign in power. I show the
judges who is right and who is wrong. Rulers rule well
with my help. I love all who love me. Those who search
for me shall surely find me. Unending riches, honor,
justice and righteousness are mine to distribute. My
gifts are better than the purest gold or sterling silver.

1 Kings 3:7, 9. Proverbs 8:15-19.

Historical Books

God gave Solomon great wisdom and understanding, and a mind with broad interests.

In fact, his wisdom excelled that of any of the wise men of the East, including those in Egypt. He was famous among all the surrounding nations.

He was the author of 3,000 proverbs and wrote 1,005 songs. He was a great naturalist, with interest in animals, birds, snakes, fish, and trees—from the great cedars of Lebanon down to the tiny hyssop which grows in cracks in the wall.

And kings from many lands sent their ambassadors to him for his advice.

How wonderful to be wise, to understand things, to be able to analyze them and interpret them.

God is always ready to give a bountiful supply of wisdom to all who ask him.

1 Kings 4:29, 30-34.
Ecclesiastes 8:1.
James 1:5.

Historical Books

O Lord, I (Solomon) have built you a lovely home on earth.

My father David wanted to build this Temple, but the Lord said not to. I have become king in my father's place, and I have built the Temple for the Name of the Lord God of Israel.

He . . . reached out his arms toward heaven, and prayed this prayer:

"Look down with favor day and night upon this Temple. Whatever the trouble is—listen to every individual's prayer concerning his private sorrow, as well as all the public prayers. Hear from heaven where you live, and forgive. Give each one whatever he deserves, for you know the hearts of all mankind."

The glory of the Lord filled the Temple. All the people . . . fell flat on the pavement, and worshiped and thanked the Lord.

1 Kings 8:13. 2 Chronicles 6:7, 8, 10, 13, 20, 28-30. 2 Chronicles 7:2, 3.

When the Queen of Sheba heard how wonderfully the Lord had blessed Solomon with wisdom, she decided to test him with some hard questions. She arrived in Jerusalem with a long train of camels carrying spices, gold and jewels; and she told him all her problems.

Solomon answered all her questions. Nothing was too

Your wisdom and prosperity are far greater

difficult for him, for the Lord gave him the right answers every time.

When she discovered how wise he really was, and how breathtaking the beauty of his palace, and how wonderful the food at this tables, and how many servants and aides he had . . . she could scarcely believe it!

1 Kings 10:7, 1-3. 2 Chronicles 9:3, 4.

than anything I've ever heard of.

Historical Books

A small mistake can outweigh much wisdom and honor.

King Solomon married many other girls besides the Egyptian princess. Many of them came from nations where idols were worshiped ... even though the Lord had clearly instructed his people not to marry into those nations because the women they married would get them started worshiping their gods. Yet Solomon did it anyway.

Sure enough, they turned his heart away from the Lord, especially in his old age.

Jehovah was very angry with Solomon about this.

Above all else, guard your affections. For they influence everything else in your life.

Ecclesiastes 10:1.
1 Kings 11:1-3, 9.
Proverbs 4:23.

Historical Books

Do all I tell you to.

King Nebuchadnezzar of Babylon ...
burned down the Temple, the palace,
and all the other houses of any worth.
He then supervised the Babylonian
army in tearing down the walls of
Jerusalem.

70 YEARS LATER
All Jews throughout the kingdom may
now return to Jerusalem to rebuild
this Temple of Jehovah. / God gave a
great desire to the leaders ... to
return to Jerusalem at once.

   Those Jews who do not go should
contribute toward the expenses of
those who do. / Some of the leaders
were able to give generously ... each
gave as much as he could.

Zechariah 3:7. 2 Kings 25:1, 9, 10. Ezra 1:3, 5, 4.
Ezra 2:68, 69.

EZRA

The actual construction of the Temple began.

Because the Lord was overseeing the entire situation, our enemies did not force us to stop building.

Don't be afraid or discouraged! Get on with rebuilding the Temple! If you do, I will certainly bless you! The future splendor of this Temple will be greater than the splendor of the first one!

So the Jewish leaders continued in their work, and they were greatly encouraged by the preaching of the prophets Haggai and Zechariah.

The Lord says, "I will make my people strong with power from me. They will go wherever they wish, and wherever they go, they will be under my personal care."

Ezra 3:8. Ezra 5:5. Zechariah 8:13, 14.
Haggai 2:8. Ezra 6:14. Zechariah 10:12.

NEHEMIAH

What a gracious and merciful God you are!

The Levite leaders called out to the people, "Stand up and praise the Lord your God, for he lives from everlasting to everlasting. Praise his glorious name! It is far greater than we can think or say."

Then Ezra prayed, "You alone are God. You have made the skies and the heavens, the earth and the seas, and everything in them. You preserve it all; and all the angels of heaven worship you.

"You led our ancestors by a pillar of cloud during the day and a pillar of fire at night so that they could find their way.

"You sent your good Spirit to instruct them, and you did not stop giving them bread from heaven or water for their thirst."

Nehemiah 9:31. Nehemiah 9:5, 6, 12, 20.

NEHEMIAH

The wall of Jerusalem is still torn down.

When I heard this . . . I (Nehemiah) spent . . . time in prayer.

"O great and awesome God who keeps his promises and is so loving and kind to those who love and obey him! Hear my prayer! Help me now as I go in and ask the king for a great favor—put it into his heart to be kind to me."

"What should be done?" the king asked.

I replied, "If it please your Majesty . . . send me to Judah to rebuild the city of my fathers!" So it was agreed.

The city officials . . . replied at once, "Good! Let's rebuild the wall!" And so the work began.

Just as water is turned into irrigation ditches, so the Lord directs the king's thoughts. He turns them wherever he wants to.

Nehemiah 1:3-5, 11.
Nehemiah 2:4, 6, 16, 18.
Proverbs 21:1.

NEHEMIAH

The wall was finished.

All the people assembled . . . and requested Ezra, their religious leader, to read to them the law of God.

All the people began sobbing when they heard the commands of the law.

Then Ezra the priest, and I as governor, and the Levites who were assisting me, said to them, "Don't cry on such a day as this! For today is a sacred day before the Lord your God—it is time to celebrate with a hearty meal, and to send presents to those in need, for the joy of the Lord is your strength."

The women and children rejoiced too, and the joy of the people of Jerusalem was heard far away!

Shout with joy before the Lord, O earth! Obey him gladly. Come before him, singing with joy.

Nehemiah 7:1. Nehemiah 8:1, 9, 10. Nehemiah 12:43. Psalm 100:1, 2.

ESTHER

O Lord, fight those fighting me. You are my mighty Protector.

King Ahasuerus appointed Haman as prime minister. The king's officials bowed before him in deep reverence. But Mordecai refused to bow.

Haman was furious, but decided not to lay hands on Mordecai alone, but to move against all of Mordecai's people, the Jews.

Haman now approached the king about the matter. The king agreed. The Jews—young and old, women and children—must all be killed.

Mordecai . . . gave Hathach a copy of the king's decree dooming all Jews, and told him to show it to Esther and to tell her . . . that she should go to the king to plead for her people.

Who can say but that God has brought you into the palace for just such a time as this?

Psalm 35:1. Psalm 71:7. Esther 3:1, 2, 5, 8, 10, 13. Esther 4:8, 14.

ESTHER

In my distress I prayed to the Lord. He is for me! How can I be afraid? What can mere man do to me?

Though it is strictly forbidden, I will go in to see the king; and if I perish, I perish.

You will not need to fight! Take your places; stand quietly and see the incredible rescue operation God will perform for you.

The king asked her, "What is your petition, Queen Esther? What do you wish?"

Queen Esther replied, "Save my life and the lives of my people. Send out a decree reversing Haman's order to destroy the Jews."

Then King Ahasuerus said . . . "Go ahead and send a message to the Jews telling them what you want to."

And in every city and province . . . the Jews were filled with joy.

Man's futile wrath will bring you glory. You will use it as an ornament!

Psalm 118:5. Esther 4:16. 2 Chronicles 20:17. Esther 7:2, 3. Esther 8:5, 8, 17. Psalm 76:10.

The purpose of his illness is . . . the glory of God.

There lived in the land of Uz a man named Job. He had a large family . . . and was immensely wealthy.

The Lord asked Satan, "Have you noticed my servant Job? He is the finest man in all the earth—a good man who fears God and will have nothing to do with evil."

"Why shouldn't he, when you pay him so well?" Satan scoffed.

"Do with him as you please," the Lord replied; "only spare his life."

Satan went out . . . and struck Job.

His suffering was too great for words. At last Job spoke . . . "Why is a man allowed to be born if God is only going to give him a hopeless life of uselessness and frustration?"

God . . . will come and pick you up, and set you firmly in place, and make you stronger than ever.

John 11:4. Job 1:1-3, 8, 9. Job 2:6, 7, 13. Job 3:1, 23. 1 Peter 5:10.

Shall we receive only pleasant things from the hand of God and never anything unpleasant?

The Lord gave me everything I had, and they were his to take away.

We can rejoice too, when we run into problems and trials for we know that they are good for us—they help us learn to be patient.

These troubles and sufferings of ours are, after all, quite small and won't last very long. Yet this short time of distress will result in God's richest blessing upon us forever and ever!

Let not your heart be troubled. You are trusting God. Now trust in me. If you love me, obey me, and I will ask the Father and he will give you another Comforter, and he will never leave you.

Job 2:10. Job 1:21. Romans 5:3. 2 Corinthians 4:17. John 14:1, 15, 16.

JOB

All nature is within your hands; you make the summer and the winter.

God stretches out heaven over empty space, and hangs the earth upon nothing. He wraps the rain in his thick clouds and the clouds are not split by the weight. He shrouds his throne with his clouds.

He sets a boundary for the ocean, yes, and a boundary for the day and for the night. The pillars of heaven tremble at his rebuke. And by his power the sea grows calm. He is skilled at crushing its pride! The heavens are made beautiful by his Spirit. He pierces the swiftly gliding serpent.

These are some of the minor things he does, merely a whisper of his power. Who then can withstand his thunder?

Psalm 74:17. Job 26:7-14.

True wisdom and power are God's.

To fear the Lord is true wisdom; to forsake evil is real understanding.

He alone knows what we should do; he understands. And how great is his might!

Trust the Lord completely. Don't ever trust yourself. In everything you do, put God first, and he will direct you and crown your efforts with success.

God is all-powerful. Who is a teacher like him?

Blessed Lord, teach me your rules. Open my eyes to see wonderful things in your Word. I am a pilgrim here on earth: how I need a map—and your commands are my chart and guide.

Job 12:13. Job 28:28. Job 12:13, 14. Proverbs 3:5, 6. Job 36:22. Psalm 119:12, 18, 19.

PSALMS

The earth belongs to God!
Everything in all the world is his!

You bound the world together so that it would never fall apart. You clothed the earth with floods of waters covering up the mountains. You spoke, and at the sound of your shout the water collected into its vast ocean beds, and mountains rose and valleys sank to the levels you decreed. And then you set a boundary for the seas, so that they would never again cover the earth. He placed springs in the valleys, and streams that gush from the mountains. They give water for all the animals to drink. There the wild donkeys quench their thirst, and the birds nest beside the streams and sing among the branches of the trees.

Psalm 24:1. Psalm 104:5-12.

PSALMS

This I declare, that he alone is my refuge, my place of safety. He is my God, and I am trusting him.

For he rescues you from every trap, and protects you from the fatal plague. He will shield you with his wings! They will shelter you. His faithful promises are your armor.

Now you don't need to be afraid of the dark any more, nor fear the dangers of the day; nor dread the plagues of darkness, nor disasters in the morning.

For the Lord says, "Because he loves me, I will rescue him. I will make him great because he trusts in my name. I will satisfy him with a full life and give him my salvation."

We live within the shadow of the Almighty, sheltered by the God who is above all gods.

Psalm 91:1-6, 14, 16.

PSALMS

Let me teach you the importance of trusting and fearing the Lord.

Do you want a long, good life? Then watch your tongue! Keep your lips from lying. Turn from all known sin and spend your time in doing good. Try to live in peace with everyone. Work hard at it.

For the eyes of the Lord are intently watching all who live good lives, and he gives attention when they cry to him. But the Lord has made up his mind to wipe out even the memory of evil men from the earth.

Yes, the Lord hears the good man when he calls to him for help, and saves him out of all his troubles.

Psalm 34:11-17.

The Lord lives on forever.

Before the mountains were
created, before the earth was
formed, you are God without
beginning or end.
You speak, and man turns
back to dust. A thousand years
are but as yesterday to you!
They are like a single hour!
We glide along the tides of
time as swiftly as a racing river,
and vanish as quickly as a
dream. We are like grass that is
green in the morning but mowed
down and withered before the
evening shadows fall.
Teach us to number our days
and recognize how few they are.
Help us to spend them as we
should.

Psalm 9:7. Psalm 90:2-6, 12.

PSALMS

Lord,
I trust in you alone.

Don't let my enemies defeat me.
Rescue me because you are the God
who always does what is right.
Answer quickly when I cry to
you; bend low and hear my whispered plea.
Be for me a great Rock of safety from my
foes. Yes, you are my Rock and my fortress;
honor your name by leading me out of this
peril. Pull me from the trap my enemies
have set for me. For you alone are strong
enough.

Hide your loved ones in the shelter of your
presence, safe beneath your hand, safe from
all conspiring men. Blessed is the Lord, for
he has shown me that his never-failing love
protects me like the walls of a fort!

Psalm 31:1-4, 20, 21.

PSALMS

Expect God to act!

Be kind and good to others. Then you will live safely here in the land and prosper, feeding in safety.

Be delighted with the Lord. Then he will give you all your heart's desires. Commit everything you do to the Lord. Trust him to help you do it and he will.

Stop your anger! Turn off your wrath. Don't fret and worry—it only leads to harm. For the wicked shall be destroyed, but those who trust the Lord shall be given every blessing.

Don't be impatient for the Lord to act! Keep traveling steadily along his pathway and in due season he will honor you with every blessing.

For the good man—the blameless, the upright, the man of peace—he has a wonderful future ahead of him. For him there is a happy ending.

Psalm 42:11. Psalm 37:3-5, 8, 34, 37.

Problems
far too big for me to solve
are piled higher than my head.

God blesses those who are kind to the poor. He helps them out of their troubles. He protects them and keeps them alive; he publicly honors them and destroys the power of their enemies. He nurses them when they are sick, and soothes their pains and worries.

"O Lord," I prayed, "be kind and heal me, for I have confessed my sins."

I waited patiently for God to help me; then he listened and heard my cry. He lifted me out of the pit of despair, out from the bog and the mire, and set my feet on a hard, firm path and steadied me as I walked along. He has given me a new song to sing, of praises to our God.

Psalm 40:12. Psalm 41:1-4. Psalm 40:1-3.

PSALMS

**It is good to say,
"Thank you" to the Lord,
to sing praises to the God
who is above all gods.**

Every morning tell him, "Thank you for your kindness," and every evening rejoice in all his faithfulness. Sing his praises, accompanied by music from the harp and lute and lyre. You have done so much for me, O Lord. No wonder I am glad! I sing for joy.

O Lord, what miracles you do! And how deep are your thoughts! Unthinking people do not understand them! No fool can comprehend this: that although the wicked flourish like weeds, there is only eternal destruction ahead of them.

But the godly shall flourish like palm trees, and grow tall as the cedars of Lebanon.

Psalm 92:1-7, 12.

Only a fool would say to himself, "There is no God."

And why does he say it? Because of his wicked heart, his dark and evil deeds. His life is corroded with sin.

God looks down from heaven, searching among all mankind to see if there is a single one who does right and really seeks for God. But all have turned their backs on him; they are filthy with sin—corrupt and rotten through and through. Not one is good, not one! Only when the Lord himself restores them can they ever be really happy again.

He is merciful and tender toward those who don't deserve it; he is slow to get angry and full of kindness and love. He never bears a grudge, nor remains angry forever. He has not punished us as we deserve for all our sins.

Psalm 53:1-3, 6. Psalm 103:8-10.

PSALMS

**None who have
faith in God
will ever be disgraced
for trusting him.**

Show me the path where I
should go, O Lord; point out the
right road for me to walk. Lead
me. Teach me. For you are the
God who gives me salvation. I
have no hope except in you.
Overlook my youthful sins,
O Lord! Look at me instead
through eyes of mercy and
forgiveness, through eyes of
everlasting love and kindness.
The Lord is good and glad to
teach the proper path to all who
go astray. He will teach the ways
that are right and best to those
who humbly turn to him. And
when we obey him, every path
he guides us on is fragrant with
his lovingkindness and his truth.

Psalm 25:3-10.

Give me common sense to apply your rules to everything I do.

Keep me far from every wrong. Help me, undeserving as I am, to obey your laws, for I have chosen to do right. I cling to your commands and follow them as closely as I can. Lord, don't let me make a mess of things. If you will only help me to want your will, then I will follow your laws even more closely.

God's laws are perfect. They protect us, make us wise, and give us joy and light. God's laws are pure, eternal, just. They are more desirable than gold. They are sweeter than honey dripping from a honeycomb. For they warn us away from harm and give success to those who obey them.

Psalm 119:125, 29-32. Psalm 19:7-11.

PROVERBS

These are the proverbs of King Solomon of Israel, David's son:

He wrote them to teach his people how to live—how to act in every circumstance, for he wanted them to be understanding, just and fair in everything they did.

"I want to make the simple-minded wise!" he said. "I want to warn young men about some problems they will face. I want those already wise to become the wiser and become leaders by exploring the depths of meaning in these nuggets of truth."

If you follow them . . . you will have a long and happy life. Learn to be wise . . . and develop good judgment and common sense! I cannot overemphasize this point.

Cling to wisdom—she will protect you. Love her—she will guard you.

Proverbs 1:1-6. Proverbs 4:4-6.

How does a man become wise?

The first step is to trust and reverence the Lord!

Give him the glory he deserves! Bring your offering and come to worship him. Worship the Lord with the beauty of holy lives.

If you want better insight and discernment, and are searching for them as you would for lost money or hidden treasure, then wisdom will be given you, and knowledge of God himself. You will soon learn the importance of reverence for the Lord and of trusting him.

For the Lord grants wisdom! His every word is a treasure of knowledge and understanding. He shows how to distinguish right from wrong, how to find the right decision every time.

Proverbs 1:7. Psalm 96:8, 9. Proverbs 2:3-6, 9.

PROVERBS

**Follow the steps
of the godly . . .
stay on the right path,
for only good men
enjoy life to the full.**

Have two goals: wisdom—that is,
knowing and doing right—and
common sense. Don't let them
slip away, for they fill you with
living energy, and are a feather
in your cap. They keep you safe
from defeat and disaster and
from stumbling off the trail.
    With them on guard you can
sleep without fear; you need not
be afraid of disaster or the plots
of wicked men.
    A life of doing right is the
wisest life there is. Carry out my
instructions; don't forget them,
for they will lead you to real
living.

Proverbs 2:20, 21. Proverbs 3:21-26.
Proverbs 4:11, 13.

PROVERBS

A wise man controls his temper.

I am Jehovah, the merciful and gracious God ... slow to anger and rich in steadfast love and truth.

Follow God's example in everything you do just as a much loved child imitates his father.

Don't let the sun go down with you still angry—get over it quickly. For when you are angry you give a mighty foothold to the devil.

Praise the Lord if you are punished for doing right! Of course, you get no credit for being patient if you are beaten for doing wrong. But if you do right and suffer for it, and are patient beneath the blows, God is well pleased.

Proverbs 14:29. Exodus 34:6. Ephesians 5:1. Ephesians 4:26, 27. 1 Peter 2:19, 20.

PROVERBS

The man of few words and settled mind is wise.

When a good man speaks, he is worth listening to, but the words of fools are a dime a dozen.

A wise man holds his tongue. Only a fool blurts out everything he knows; that only leads to sorrow and trouble.

Those who love to talk will suffer the consequences. Men have died for saying the wrong thing!

Self-control means controlling the tongue! A quick retort can ruin everything.

The tongue is a small thing, but what enormous damage it can do.

Proverbs 17:27. Proverbs 10:20, 14.
Proverbs 18:21. Proverbs 13:3. James 3:5.

He grants good sense
to the godly—his saints.
He is their shield,
protecting them and
guarding their pathway.

The steps of good men are directed by
the Lord. He delights in each step they
take. If they fall it isn't fatal, for the
Lord holds them with his hand.

The good man does not escape all
troubles—he has them too. But the
Lord helps him in each and every one.

And we know that all that happens
to us is working for our good if we
love God and are fitting into his plans.

For the Lord watches over all the plans
and paths of godly men, but the paths
of the godless lead to doom.

We have the Lord our God to fight
our battles for us! The Lord is a
warrior—Yes, Jehovah is his name.

Proverbs 2:7, 8. Psalm 37:23, 24. Psalm 34:19.
Romans 8:28. Psalm 1:6. 2 Chronicles 32:8.
Exodus 15:3.

PROVERBS

All who listen to me shall live in peace and safety, unafraid.

We live within the shadow of the Almighty, sheltered by the God who is above all gods.

His faithful promises are your armor. He who harms you sticks his finger in Jehovah's eye!

God is our refuge and strength, a tested help in times of trouble. And so we need not fear even if the world blows up, and the mountains crumble into the sea.

Jesus immediately spoke to them, reassuring them. "Don't be afraid!" he said.

Proverbs 1:33. Psalm 91:1, 4.
Zechariah 2:8. Psalm 46:1, 2.
Matthew 14:27.

PROVERBS

You can sleep without fear.

You need not be afraid of disaster ... for the Lord is with you; he protects you.

Don't worry about anything; instead, pray about everything; tell God your needs and don't forget to thank him for his answers. If you do this you will experience God's peace, which is far more wonderful than the human mind can understand. His peace will keep your thoughts and your hearts quiet and at rest as you trust in Christ Jesus.

I will lie down in peace and sleep, for though I am alone, O Lord, you will keep me safe.

Proverbs 3:24-26. Philippians 4:6, 7. Psalm 4:8.

PROVERBS

Trust the Lord completely; don't ever trust yourself.

In everything you do, put God first, and he will direct you and crown your efforts with success.

I will instruct you (says the Lord) and guide you along the best pathway for your life. I will advise you and watch your progress. Don't be like a senseless horse or mule that has to have a bit in its mouth to keep it in line!

The Lord will guide you continually, and satisfy you with all good things, and keep you healthy too. And you will be like a well-watered garden, like an ever-flowing spring. Abiding love surrounds those who trust in the Lord.

Proverbs 3:5, 6. Psalm 32:8, 9. Isaiah 58:11. Psalm 32:10.

PROVERBS

Don't refuse to accept criticism; get all the help you can. The advice of a wise man refreshes like water from a mountain spring. Those accepting it become aware of the pitfalls on ahead.

Obey your father and your mother. Tie their instructions around your finger so you won't forget. Take to heart all of their advice.

For their advice is a beam of light directed into the dark corners of your mind to warn you of danger and to give you a good life.

Watch your step. Stick to the path and be safe. Don't sidetrack, pull back your foot from danger.

Give your parents joy!

Proverbs 23:25, 12. Proverbs 13:14.
Proverbs 6:20, 21, 23. Proverbs 4:26, 27.

PROVERBS

**Wise men are praised
for their wisdom;
fools are despised
for their folly.**

A FOOL

- ☐ thinks he needs no advice
- ☐ is quick-tempered
- ☐ displays his foolishness
- ☐ attempts to fool himself and
  won't face facts
- ☐ plunges ahead with great
  confidence.

A WISE MAN

- ☐ listens to others
- ☐ stays cool when insulted
- ☐ doesn't display his knowledge
- ☐ looks ahead
- ☐ is cautious and avoids
  danger.

Be with wise men and become
wise. Be with evil men and
become evil.

Proverbs 14:24. Proverbs 12:15, 16, 23.
Proverbs 14:8, 16. Proverbs 13:20.

PROVERBS

If you give little, you will get little. A farmer who plants just a few seeds will get only a small crop, but if he plants much, he will reap much. God will give you much so that you can give away much.

Every Sunday each of you should put aside something from what you have earned during the week.

For if you give, you will get! Your gift will return to you in full and overflowing measure, pressed down, shaken together to make room for more, and running over. Whatever measure you use to give—large or small—will be used to measure what is given back to you.

It is possible to give away and become richer!

Proverbs 3:9.
2 Corinthians 9:6.
2 Corinthians 9:11.
1 Corinthians 16:2. Luke 6:38.
Proverbs 11:24.

Honor the Lord by giving him the first part of all your income.

Ecclesiastes

God has already given you everything you need.

No matter how much we see, we are never satisfied. No matter how much we hear, we are not content.

History merely repeats itself. Nothing is truly new; it has all been done before.

But as for me, my contentment is . . . in seeing you and knowing all is well between us. And when I awake in heaven, I will be fully satisfied, for I will see you face to face.

God's peace . . . far more wonderful than the human mind can understand. I have learned the secret of contentment in every situation.

The answer lies in Christ.

1 Corinthians 3:21. Ecclesiastes 1:8, 9.
Psalm 17:15. Philippians 4:7, 12. 1 Timothy 3:16.

APRIL 22

Ecclesiastes

FROM ETERNITY TO

Though God has planted eternity in the hearts of men, even so, man cannot see the whole scope of God's work from beginning to end.

God's ways are as mysterious as the pathway of the wind, and as the manner in which a human spirit is infused into the little body of a baby while it is yet in its mother's womb.

Ecclesiastes

ETERNITY I AM GOD.

We can see and understand only a little about God now, as if we were peering at his reflection in a poor mirror. But someday we are going to see him in his completeness, face to face. Now all that I know is hazy and blurred, but then I will see everything clearly, just as clearly as God sees into my heart right now.

Isaiah 43:13. Ecclesiastes 3:11. Ecclesiastes 11:5. 1 Corinthians 13:12.

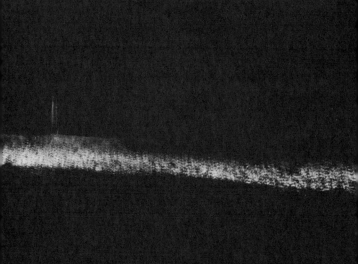

Ecclesiastes

The swiftest person does not always win the race, nor the strongest man the battle. Wise men are often poor, and skillful men are not necessarily famous. Stop fooling yourselves. If you count yourself above average in intelligence, as judged by this world's standards, you had better put this all aside and be a fool rather than let it hold you back from the true wisdom from above.

For the wisdom of this world is foolishness to God. And . . . in the book of Psalms, we are told that the Lord knows full well how the human mind reasons, and how foolish and futile it is.

1 Corinthians 3:21. Ecclesiastes 9:11.
1 Corinthians 3:18-20.

Don't be proud of following the wise men of this world.

Here is my final conclusion.

Fear God and obey his commandments, for this is the entire duty of man. For God will judge us for everything we do, including every hidden thing, good or bad.

It is a wonderful thing to be alive! If a person lives to be very old, let him rejoice in every day of life.

It's wonderful to be young! Enjoy every minute of it! But remember that youth, with a whole life before it, can make serious mistakes.

Never forget the things I've taught you. If you want a long and satisfying life, closely follow my instructions. Hold these virtues tightly. Write them deep within your heart.

Ecclesiastes 12:13, 14. Ecclesiastes 11:7, 9, 10. Proverbs 3:1-3.

Song of Solomon

Solomon now moved his wife . . . to the new palace he had built for her.

THE GIRL: The king has brought me into his palace. How happy we will be!

KING SOLOMON: You have ravished my heart, my lovely one, my bride. I am overcome by one glance of your eyes, by a single bead of your necklace. The perfume of your love is more fragrant than all the richest spices.

THE GIRL: Seal me in your heart with permanent betrothal, for love is strong as death and jealousy is as cruel as Sheol. It flashes fire, the very flame of Jehovah. Many waters cannot quench the flame of love, neither can the floods drown it. If a man tried to buy it with everything he owned, he couldn't do it.

2 Chronicles 8:11. Song of Solomon 1:4. Song of Solomon 4:9, 10.
Song of Solomon 8:6, 7.

ISAIAH

Your country lies in ruins.
Your cities are burned.

These are the messages that came to Isaiah. In these messages God showed him what was going to happen to Judah and Jerusalem in the days ahead.

Listen, O heaven and earth, to what the Lord is saying:

The children I raised and cared for so long and tenderly have turned against me. No matter what I do for them, they still don't care. Oh, what a sinful nation they are!

Haven't you had enough of punishment? . . . Must you forever rebel?

Oh, wash yourselves! Be clean! Let me no longer see you doing all these wicked things. Quit your evil ways.

Come, let's talk this over! says the Lord. If you will only let me help you, if you will only obey, then I will make you rich!

Isaiah 1:7, 1-5, 16, 18, 19.

ISAIAH

In Jehovah is all my righteousness and strength.

The year King Uzziah died I (Isaiah) saw the Lord! He was sitting on a lofty throne, and the Temple was filled with his glory. Hovering about him were mighty, six-winged seraphs. In a great antiphonal chorus they sang,

HOLY
HOLY
HOLY

is the Lord of Hosts. The whole earth is filled with his glory." Such singing it was!

Then I said, "My doom is sealed, for I am a foul-mouthed sinner . . . and I have looked upon the King, the Lord of heaven's armies."

Let all the world look to me for salvation! For I am God; there is no other. I have sworn by myself and I will never go back on my word, for it is true—that every knee in all the world shall bow to me, and every tongue shall swear allegiance to my name.

Isaiah 45:24. Isaiah 6:1-5. Isaiah 45:22, 23.

ISAIAH

The glory of the Lord will be seen by all mankind together.

Your God is coming! Yes, the Lord God is coming with mighty power. He will rule with awesome strength. Who else has held the oceans in his hands and measured off the heavens with his ruler? Who else knows the weight of all the earth and weighs the mountains and the hills? Who can advise the Spirit of the Lord or be his teacher or give him counsel? Has he ever needed anyone's advice? Did he need instruction as to what is right and best? No, for all the peoples of the world are nothing in comparison with him—they are but a drop in the bucket, dust on the scales. He picks up the islands as though they had no weight at all.

Isaiah 40:5,9,10,12-15.

ISAIAH

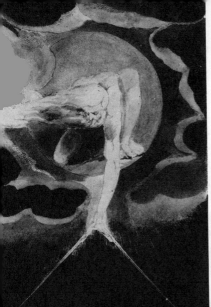

How can we describe God? With what can we compare him?

William Blake, *The Ancient of Days*,
Lessing J. Rosenwald Collection, Library of Congress

It is God who sits above the circle of the earth.
The people below must seem to him like
grasshoppers! He is the one who stretches out
the heavens like a curtain and makes his tent
from them.

He dooms the great men of the world and
brings them all to naught. They hardly get
started, barely take root, when he blows on
them and their work withers and the wind
carries them off like straw.

No one can fathom the depths of his
understanding. He gives power to the tired and
worn out, and strength to the weak. Even the
youths shall be exhausted, and the young men
will all give up. But they that wait upon the
Lord shall renew their strength.

Isaiah 40:18,22-24,28-31.

ISAIAH

Don't fear anything except the Lord of the armies of heaven! If you fear him, you need fear nothing else. He will be your safety.

Those who still reject me are like the restless sea, which is never still, but always churns up mire and dirt. There is no peace, says my God, for them!

Seek the Lord while you can find him. Call upon him now while he is near.

Let men cast off their wicked deeds. Let them banish from their minds the very thought of doing wrong! Let them turn to the Lord that he may have mercy upon them, and to our God, for he will abundantly pardon!

Isaiah 55:9. Isaiah 8:13, 14. Isaiah 57:20, 21. Isaiah 55:6, 7.

Just as the heavens are higher than the earth, so are my ways higher than yours.

ISAIAH

Jesus the Messiah ... there is salvation in no one else.

In our eyes there was no attractiveness at all, nothing to make us want him.

We despised him and rejected him—a man of sorrows, acquainted with bitterest grief. We turned our backs on him and looked the other way when he went by. He was despised and we didn't care.

He was oppressed and he was afflicted, yet he never said a word. He was brought as a lamb to the slaughter; and as a sheep before her shearers is dumb, so he stood silent before the ones condemning him.

From prison and trial they led him away to his death. He was buried like a criminal in a rich man's grave. He had done no wrong, and had never spoken an evil word.

He died for our sins.

Acts 4:11, 12. Isaiah 53:2, 3, 7-9. Romans 4:25.

ISAIAH

I will tell you the future before it happens.

I am the First and Last; there is no other God. Who else can tell you what is going to happen in the days ahead? For see, I am creating new heavens and a new earth—so wonderful that no one will even think about the old ones anymore.

No longer will babies die when only a few days old. No longer will men be considered old at 100!

The wolf and lamb shall feed together, the lion shall eat straw as the ox does, and poisonous snakes shall strike no more!

In that day the deaf will hear the words of a book, and out of their gloom and darkness the blind will see my plans.

Isaiah 42:9. Isaiah 44:6, 7. Isaiah 65:17, 20, 25. Isaiah 29:18.

JEREMIAH

You saw me before I was born and scheduled each day of my life before I began to breathe.

The Lord said to (Jeremiah), "I knew you before you were formed within your mother's womb; before you were born I sanctified you and appointed you as my spokesman to the world."

"O Lord God," I said, "I can't do that! I'm far too young! I'm only a youth!"

"Don't say that," he replied, "for you will go wherever I send you and speak whatever I tell you to. And don't be afraid of the people, for I, the Lord, will be with you and see you through."

Then he touched my mouth and said, "See, I have put my words in your mouth! Today your work begins, to warn the nations and the kingdoms of the world."

Psalm 139:16. Jeremiah 1:4-10.

JEREMIAH

Listen to this message from God.

Don't fool yourselves! Do you really think you can steal, murder, commit adultery, lie, and worship Baal and all of those new gods of yours, and then come here and stand before me in my Temple and chant, "We are saved!" —only to go right back to all these evil things again?

Am I the one that they are hurting? asks the Lord. Most of all they hurt themselves, to their own shame.

It wasn't offerings and sacrifices I wanted from your fathers when I led them out of Egypt. That was not the point of my command. But what I told them was: Obey me and I will be your God and you shall be my people. Only do as I say and all shall be well!

Jeremiah 7:2, 8-10, 19, 22, 23.

JEREMIAH

O Lord, there is no other god like you.

Don't act like the people who make horoscopes and try to read their fate and future in the stars! Don't be frightened by predictions such as theirs, for it is all a pack of lies.

Can the living find out the future from the dead? Why not ask your God?

They cut down a tree and carve an idol . . . and there stands their god like a helpless scarecrow in a garden!

The wisest of men who worship idols are altogether stupid and foolish.

The Lord is the only true God, the living God, the everlasting King.

Say this to those who worship other gods . . . Our God formed the earth by his power and intelligence . . . It is his voice that echoes in the thunder.

Jeremiah 10:6, 2, 3. Isaiah 8:19.
Jeremiah 10:3, 5, 8, 10-13.

JEREMIAH

O Lord . . .
all who turn away
from you . . .
are registered for earth
and not for glory.

The Lord says: Cursed is the man who puts his trust in mortal man and turns his heart away from God. He is like a stunted shrub in the desert, with no hope for the future; he lives on the salt-encrusted plains in the barren wilderness; good times pass him by forever.

But blessed is the man who trusts in the Lord and has made the Lord his hope and confidence. He is like a tree planted along a riverbank, with its roots reaching deep into the water—a tree not bothered by the heat nor worried by long months of drought. Its leaves stay green and it goes right on producing all its luscious fruit.

Jeremiah 17:13, 5-8.

JEREMIAH

I know the plans I have for you, says the Lord.
They are plans for good and not for evil.

I . . . found the potter working at his wheel. But the jar that he was forming didn't turn out as he wished, so he kneaded it into a lump and started again.

Then the Lord said . . . "As the clay is in the potter's hand, so are you in my hand."

Shall the axe boast greater power than the man who uses it? Is the saw greater than the man who saws? Can a rod strike unless a hand is moving it? Can a cane walk by itself?

The Lord . . . who can change his plans? When his hand moves, who can stop him?

Jeremiah 29:11. Jeremiah 18:3-6. Isaiah 10-15. Isaiah 14:27.

JEREMIAH

A beautiful palace does not make a great king!

Men judge by outward appearances, but I look at a man's thoughts and intentions.

Why did . . . Josiah reign so long? Because he was just and fair in all his dealings. That is why God blessed him. He saw to it that justice and help were given the poor and the needy and all went well for him. This is how a man lives close to God.

The heart is the most deceitful thing there is, and desperately wicked. No one can really know how bad it is! Only the Lord knows! He searches all hearts and examines deepest motives so he can give to each person his right reward, according to his deeds— how he has lived.

Jeremiah 22:15. 1 Samuel 16:7. Jeremiah 22:15, 16. Jeremiah 17:9, 10.

Lamentations

Is any sorrow like my sorrow?

Jerusalem's streets, once thronged with people, are silent now. Like a widow broken with grief, she sits alone in her mourning. She, once queen of nations, is now a slave.

The elders of Jerusalem sit upon the ground in silence, clothed in sackcloth, they throw dust upon their heads in sorrow and despair.

Little children and tiny babies are fainting and dying in the streets.

In all the world has there ever been such sorrow? Your wound is deep as the sea. Who can heal you?

Rise in the night and cry to your God. Pour out your hearts like water to the Lord.

O Lord, forever you remain the same! Turn us around and bring us back to you again! That is our only hope!

Lamentations 1:12, 1. Lamentations 2:10, 11, 13, 19.
Lamentations 5:19, 21.

Lamentations

**To all who mourn in Israel
he will give:
beauty for ashes;
joy instead of mourning;
praise instead of heaviness.**

O Lord, all peace and all prosperity have long since gone, for you have taken them away. I have forgotten what enjoyment is. All hope is gone. My strength has turned to water, for the Lord has left me.

Yet there is one ray of hope: his compassion never ends. It is only the Lord's mercies that have kept us from complete destruction. Great is his faithfulness; his lovingkindness begins afresh each day.

My soul claims the Lord as my inheritance; therefore I will hope in him. The Lord is wonderfully good to those who wait for him, to those who seek for him.

Isaiah 61:3. Lamentations 3:17, 18, 21-25.

Lamentations

It is good for a young man to be under discipline, for
it causes him to sit apart in silence beneath the Lord's
demands, to lie face downward in the dust;
then at last there is hope for him.
Let him turn the other cheek to those who strike him,
and accept their awful insults,
for the Lord will not abandon him forever.
Although God gives him grief, yet he will show
compassion too, according to the greatness of his
lovingkindness. For he does not enjoy afflicting men
and causing sorrow.
Why then should we, mere humans as we are, murmur
and complain when punished for our sins? Let us . . .
repent and turn again to the Lord.

Romans 5:20. Lamentations 3:27-33, 39,40.

**The more
we see our
sinfulness,
the more
we see God's
abounding
grace
forgiving us.**

EZEKIEL

light the path a

тење покајања за ipo

O EARTH, EARTH, EARTH!
HEAR THE WORD OF THE LORD!

Let my words sink deep into your own heart first. Listen to them carefully for yourself. Then afterward go to your people in exile, and whether or not they will listen, tell them: This is what the Lord God says!

As the rain and snow come down from heaven and stay upon the ground to water the earth, and cause the grain to grow and to produce seed for the farmer and bread for the hungry, so also is my Word.

I send it out and it always produces fruit. It shall accomplish all I want it to, and prosper everywhere I send it.

Blessed are all who hear the Word of God and put it into practice.

Jeremiah 22:29. Ezekiel 3:10, 11. Isaiah 55:10. Luke 11:28.

EZEKIEL

God is closely watching you, and he weighs carefully everything you do.

I know everything you think—every thought that comes into your minds.

Don't try to disclaim responsibility by saying you didn't know about it. For God, who knows all hearts, knows yours, and he knows you knew! And he will reward everyone according to his deeds.

The righteous person will be rewarded for his own goodness and the wicked person for his wickedness. But if a wicked person turns away from all his sins and begins to obey (God's) laws and do what is just and right . . . all his past sins will be forgotten, and he shall live because of his goodness.

Turn from your sins while there is yet time. Put them behind you and receive a new heart and a new spirit.

Proverbs 5:21. Ezekiel 11:5. Proverbs 24:12. Ezekiel 18:20-22, 30, 31.

EZEKIEL

You shall be my people and I will be your God.

The Lord God says: I will search and find my sheep. I will be like a shepherd looking for his flock. I will find my sheep and rescue them from all the places they were scattered.

I myself will be the Shepherd of my sheep, and cause them to lie down in peace, the Lord God says. I will seek my lost ones, those who strayed away, and bring them safely home again.

I will put splints and bandages upon their broken limbs and heal the sick.

If you had a hundred sheep and one of them strayed away and was lost in the wilderness, wouldn't you leave the ninety-nine others to go and search for the lost one until you found it?

Ezekiel 36:28.
Ezekiel 34:11, 12, 15, 16.
Luke 15:3, 4.

DANIEL

The Lord grants wisdom!

King Nebuchadnezzar ... ordered Ashpenaz ... to select some of the Jewish youths ... to teach them the Chaldean language and literature. Daniel, Hananiah, Misha-el, and Azariah were four of the young men chosen.

God gave these four youths great ability to learn and they soon mastered all the literature and science of the time.

In all matters requiring information and balanced judgment, the king found these young men's advice ten times better than that of all the skilled magicians and wise astrologers in his realm.

Wisdom gives: a long, good life, riches, honor, pleasure, peace.

Proverbs 2:6. Daniel 1:1, 3, 4, 6, 17, 20. Proverbs 3:16, 17.

DANIEL

The godly shall flourish like palm trees.

Daniel made up his mind not to eat the food and wine given to them by the king. He asked the superintendent for permission to eat other things instead . . . and suggested a ten-day diet of only vegetables and water.

At the end of the ten days, Daniel and his three friends looked healthier and better nourished than the youths who had been eating the food supplied by the king!

Food isn't everything . . . real life comes by obeying every command of God.

Happy are those who are strong in the Lord, who want above all else to follow your steps. For Jehovah God is our Light and our Protector. He gives us grace and glory. No good thing will he withhold from those who walk along his paths.

Psalm 92:12. Daniel 1:8, 12, 15.
Deuteronomy 8:3. Psalm 84:5, 11.

DANIEL

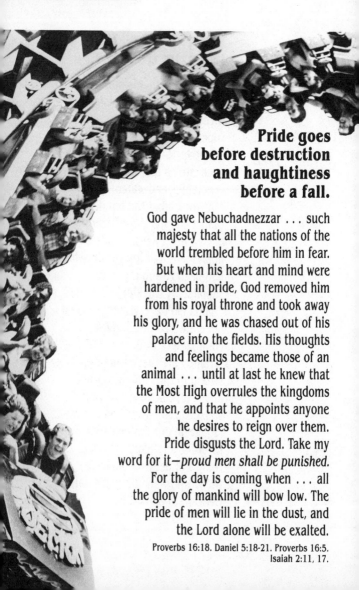

**Pride goes
before destruction
and haughtiness
before a fall.**

God gave Nebuchadnezzar ... such
majesty that all the nations of the
world trembled before him in fear.
But when his heart and mind were
hardened in pride, God removed him
from his royal throne and took away
his glory, and he was chased out of his
palace into the fields. His thoughts
and feelings became those of an
animal ... until at last he knew that
the Most High overrules the kingdoms
of men, and that he appoints anyone
he desires to reign over them.
Pride disgusts the Lord. Take my
word for it—*proud men shall be punished.*
For the day is coming when ... all
the glory of mankind will bow low. The
pride of men will lie in the dust, and
the Lord alone will be exalted.

Proverbs 16:18. Daniel 5:18-21. Proverbs 16:5.
Isaiah 2:11, 17.

DANIEL

God . . . alone has all wisdom and all power.

World events are under his control. He removes kings and sets others on their thrones. He gives wise men their wisdom, and scholars their intelligence. He reveals profound mysteries beyond man's understanding.

He knows all hidden things, for he is light, and darkness is no obstacle to him.

Who can advise the Spirit of the Lord or be his teacher or give him counsel? Has he ever needed anyone's advice?

Who would not fear you, O King of Nations? (And that title belongs to you alone!) Among all the wise men of the earth and in all the kingdoms of the world there isn't anyone like you.

Daniel 2:20-22. Isaiah 40:13, 14. Jeremiah 10:7.

DANIEL

Because he bends down and listens, I will pray as long as I breathe.

I will pray morning, noon and night, pleading aloud with God; and he will hear and answer. Though the tide of battle runs strongly against me, for so many are fighting me, yet he will rescue me.

Daniel . . . went home and knelt down as usual in his upstairs bedroom, with its windows open toward Jerusalem, and prayed three times a day, just as he always had, giving thanks to his God.

For the eyes of the Lord are intently watching all who live good lives, and he gives attention when they cry to him.

Pray all the time. Ask God for anything in line with the Holy Spirit's wishes. Plead with him, reminding him of your needs, and keep praying earnestly for all Christians everywhere.

Psalm 116:2. Psalm 55:17, 18. Daniel 6:10. Psalm 34:15. Ephesians 6:18.

DANIEL

God's plans are unshakable.

Belshazzar the king . . . . saw the fingers of a man's hand writing on the . . . wall.

"Call for this man, Daniel . . . for his mind is filled with divine knowledge and understanding. He can interpret dreams, explain riddles, and solve knotty problems."

Daniel answered . . . "You have not praised the God who gives you the breath of life and controls your destiny!

"And so God sent those fingers to write this message:

MENE
(God has numbered the days of your reign.)

TEKEL
(You have been weighed in God's balances and have failed the test.)

PARSIN
(Your kingdom will be divided and given to the Medes and Persians.)"

The Most High God . . . gives power to anyone he chooses. No wonder men everywhere fear him! For he is not impressed by the world's wisest men!

Daniel 11:36. Daniel 5:1, 5, 12, 17, 23, 24-28. Daniel 4:25.
Job 37:24.

HOSEA

O people of Israel.
The Lord has filed
a lawsuit against you.

There is no faithfulness, no kindness, no knowledge of God in your land. You swear and lie and kill and steal and commit adultery. There is violence everywhere, with one murder after another.

That is why your land is not producing. It is filled with sadness, and all living things grow sick and die. The animals, the birds, and even the fish begin to disappear. Your harvests will be small; your grapes will blight upon the vine.

Don't be misled; remember that you can't ignore God and get away with it: a man will always reap just the kind of crop he sows!

Whoever is wise, let him understand these things. Whoever is intelligent, let him listen.

Hosea 4:1-3. Hosea 9:2. Galatians 6:7. Hosea 14:9.

HOSEA

They are asking a piece of wood to tell them what to do.

"Divine Truth" comes to them through tea leaves.

My people mingle with the heathen, picking up their evil ways; thus they become as good-for-nothing as a half-baked cake.

I have helped them, and made them strong, yet now they turn against me.

They look everywhere except to heaven, to the Most High God. They are like a crooked bow that always misses targets. Their leaders will perish by the sword of the enemy for their insolence to me.

My fury burns against you. How long will it be before one honest man is found among you?

Hosea 4:12. Hosea 7:8, 15, 16. Hosea 8:5.

HOSEA

As soon as trouble comes, they will search for me and say:

"Come, let us return to the Lord; it is he who has torn us—he will heal us. He has wounded—he will bind us up. In just a couple of days, or three at the most, he will set us on our feet again, to live in his kindness!

"Oh, that we might know the Lord! Let us press on to know him, and he will respond to us as surely as the coming of dawn or the rain of early spring."

O Ephraim and Judah, what shall I do with you? For your love vanishes like morning clouds, and disappears like dew.

I don't want your sacrifices—I want your love. I don't want your offerings—I want you to know me.

Hosea 5:15. Hosea 6:1-4, 6.

HOSEA

Stay away from idols! I am living and strong!

I look after you and care for you.
I am like an evergreen tree,
yielding my fruit to you
throughout the year. My mercies
never fail.
Plant the good seeds of
righteousness and you will reap
a crop of my love. Plow the hard
ground of your hearts, for now is
the time to seek the Lord, that
he may come and shower
salvation upon you.
Oh, come back to God. Live by
the principles of love and
justice, and always be expecting
much from him, your God.
Whoever is wise, let him
understand these things.
Whoever is intelligent, let him
listen. For the paths of the Lord
are true and right, and good
men walk along them.
But sinners trying it will fail.

Hosea 14:8. Hosea 10:12. Hosea 12:6.
Hosea 14:9.

JOEL

Rejoice in the Lord your God! For the rains he sends are tokens of forgiveness.

Once more the autumn rains will come, as well as those of spring. The threshing floors will pile high again with wheat, and the presses overflow with olive oil and wine. And I will give you back the crops the locusts ate—my great destroying army that I sent against you. Once again you will have all the food you want.

What happiness for those whose guilt has been forgiven! What joys when sins are covered over! What relief for those who have confessed their sins and God has cleared their record.

Who can forget the wonders he performs—deeds of mercy and of grace? He gives food to those who trust him; he never forgets his promises.

Joel 2:23-26. Psalm 32:1, 2. Psalm 111:4.

JOEL

**The
Day
of the
Lord
is near.**

The sun and moon will be darkened and the stars
withdraw their light. The Lord shouts from his Temple in
Jerusalem and the earth and sky begin to shake. But to
his people Israel, the Lord will be very gentle. He is their
Refuge and Strength.

God is our refuge and strength, a tested help in times
of trouble. And so we need not fear even if the world
blows up, and the mountains crumble into the sea. Let
the oceans roar and foam; let the mountains tremble!

The Commander of the heavenly armies is here
among us!

He, the God of Jacob has come to rescue us!

Joel 3:14-16. Psalm 46:1-3, 11.

AMOS

The people . . . have sinned again and again and I will not forget it.

I will not leave them unpunished any more.

"My people have forgotten what it means to do right," says the Lord. "Their beautiful homes are full of the loot from their thefts and banditry."

Prepare to meet your God in judgment, Israel. For you are dealing with the one who formed the mountains and made the winds, and knows your every thought.

He closely watches everything that happens here on earth.

Amos 1:9. Amos 3:10.
Amos 4:12, 13.
Psalm 11:4.

Seek me—and live.

Seek the Lord and live.
Seek him who created the Seven
Stars and the constellation Orion, who
turns darkness into morning, and day
into night, who calls forth the water
from the ocean and pours it out as
rain upon the land.

Be good, flee evil—and live! Then
the Lord God of Hosts will truly be
your Helper, as you have claimed he is.

Happy is the man who has the God
of Jacob as his helper, whose hope is
in the Lord his God—the God who
made both earth and heaven, the seas
and everything in them. He is the God
who keeps every promise.

Eternal life is in him and this life gives
light to all mankind.

Amos 5:4, 6, 8, 14. Psalm 146:5. John 1:4.

OBADIAH

Your acts will boomerang upon your heads.

You deserted Israel in his time of need. You stood aloof, refusing to lift a finger to help him when invaders carried off his wealth and divided Jerusalem among them by lot. You were as one of his enemies. As you have done to Israel, so will it be done to you.

Knowing what is right to do and then not doing it is sin. Don't try to disclaim responsibility by saying you didn't know about it. For God, who knows all hearts, knows yours, and he knows you knew! And he will reward everyone according to his deeds. Only the Lord knows! He searches all hearts and examines deepest motives.

Obadiah 1:15, 11, 15. James 4:17. Proverbs 24:11, 12. Jeremiah 17:10.

JONAH

The Lord sent this message to Jonah . . . "Go to the great city of Nineveh."

But Jonah was afraid to go and ran away from the Lord.

What right have you to fear mere mortal men, who wither like the grass and disappear? And yet you have no fear of God, your Maker?

Don't fear anything except the Lord of the armies of heaven! If you fear him, you need fear nothing else. He will be your safety.

The Lord is good and glad to teach the proper path to all who go astray. He will teach the ways that are right and best to those who humbly turn to him. Where is the man who fears the Lord? God will teach him how to choose the best.

Jonah 1:1-3. Isaiah 51:12. Isaiah 8:13, 14. Psalm 25:8, 12.

JONAH

How stupid I am.

Jonah ... found a ship leaving for Tarshish. He ... went on board, and climbed down into the dark hold of the ship to hide there from the Lord. / *Can anyone hide from me?*

As the ship was sailing along, suddenly the Lord flung a terrific wind over the sea, causing a great storm. / *You have brought this on yourselves by rebelling against the Lord your God.*

They picked up Jonah and threw him overboard into the raging sea ... the Lord had arranged for a great fish to swallow Jonah. / *Your ways have brought this down upon you. It is a bitter dose of your own medicine.*

Then Jonah prayed ... from inside the fish: "I cried to the Lord and he answered me." / *His compassion is intertwined with everything he does.*

Psalm 69:5. Jonah 1:3. Jeremiah 23:24. Jonah 1:4.
Jeremiah 2:17. Jonah 1:15, 17. Jeremiah 4:18.
Jonah 2:1, 2. Psalm 145:9.

JONAH

I thought about the wrong direction in which I was headed.

When I had lost all hope, I turned my thoughts once more to the Lord. And my earnest prayer went to you in your holy Temple. I will never worship anyone but you! For how can I thank you enough for all you have done? I will surely fulfill my promises. For my deliverance comes from the Lord alone.

And the Lord ordered the fish to spit up Jonah on the beach, and it did.

Lord, if you keep in mind our sins then who can ever get an answer to his prayers? But you forgive! What an awesome thing this is!

The Lord our God is merciful, and pardons even those who have rebelled against him. Where is another God like you?

Psalm 119:59. Jonah 2:7, 9, 10. Psalm 130:3, 4. Daniel 9:9. Micah 7:18.

JONAH

Jonah obeyed
and went to Nineveh.

The very first day when Jonah entered the city and began to preach, the people repented. Jonah shouted to the crowds that gathered around him, "Forty days from now Nineveh will be destroyed!" And they believed him and declared a fast. Perhaps even yet God will decide to let us live, and will hold back his fierce anger from destroying us.

And when God saw that they had put a stop to their evil ways, he abandoned his plan to destroy them, and didn't carry it through.

You cannot stay angry with your people, for you love to be merciful. Once again you will have compassion on us.

How kind he is! How good he is! So merciful, this God of ours!

Jonah 3:3-5, 9, 10. Micah 7:18, 19. Psalm 116:5.

JONAH

This change of plans made Jonah very angry.

He complained to the Lord about it. "This is exactly what I thought you'd do, Lord, when . . . you first told me to come here. That's why I ran away to Tarshish. For I knew you were a gracious God, merciful, slow to get angry, and full of kindness. I knew how easily you could cancel your plans for destroying these people."

Then the Lord said . . . "And why shouldn't I feel sorry for a great city like Nineveh with its 120,000 people in utter spiritual darkness?

"Do you think I like to see the wicked die?" asks the Lord. "Of course not! I only want him to turn from his wicked ways and live."

His compassion never ends.

Jonah 4:1, 2, 10, 11. Ezekiel 18:23. Lamentations 3:22.

MICAH

ATTENTION!

These are messages from the Lord . . . to Samaria and Judah, and came to Micah in the form of visions.

Let all the peoples of the world listen. For the Lord in his holy Temple has made accusations against you!

And why is this happening? Because of the sins of Israel and Judah.

What sins? Idolatry and oppression . . . You want a certain piece of land, or someone else's house (though it is all he has); you take it by fraud and threats and violence. You steal the shirts right off the backs of those who trusted you.

Therefore I will wound you! I will make your hearts miserable for all your sins.

Micah 1:2, 1, 2, 5. Micah 2:2, 8. Micah 6:13.

MICAH

His threats are for your good, to get you on the path again.

Don't be angry when the Lord punishes you. Don't be discouraged when he has to show you where you are wrong. For when he punishes you, it proves that he loves you. When he whips you it proves you are really his child. Let God train you, for he is doing what any loving father does for his children. Whoever heard of a son who was never corrected?

So he helps us by punishing us. This makes us follow his paths.

God's correction is always right and for our best good, that we may share his holiness.

The time will come, O Israel, when I will gather you . . . and bring you together again like sheep in a fold.

Micah 2:7. Hebrews 12:5-7. Psalm 94:12. Hebrews 12:10. Micah 2:12.

MICAH

Your King will go before you—
the Lord leads on.

The time will come, O Israel, when I will gather you.

His anger lasts a moment, his favor lasts for life! Weeping may go on all night, but in the morning there is joy.

I look to the Lord for his help; I wait for God to save me; he will hear me. I will be patient while the Lord punishes me, for I have sinned against him. God will bring me out of my darkness into the light, and I will see his goodness.

I am listening carefully to all the Lord is saying—for he speaks peace to his people, his saints, if they will only stop their sinning.

Micah 2:13, 12. Psalm 30:5. Micah 7:7, 9. Psalm 85:8.

NAHUM

Who can stand before an angry God?

Nineveh, you are finished! You are already surrounded by enemy armies! Sound the alarm! The Lord of Hosts has turned against you . . . never again will you rule the earth.

All this because Nineveh sold herself to the enemies of God. The beautiful and faithless city, mistress of deadly charms, enticed the nations with her beauty, then taught them all to worship her false gods, bewitching people everywhere.

You pronounce sentence on them from heaven; the earth trembles and stands silently before you.

This mighty King is determined to give justice. Fairness is the touchstone of everything he does.

Nahum 1:6. Nahum 2:1, 13. Nahum 3:4. Psalm 76:8. Psalm 99:4.

ΠAHUM

**Lord God,
to whom
vengeance
belongs,
let your glory
shine out.**

God is jealous over those he loves. That is why he takes vengeance on those who hurt them. He furiously destroys their enemies. He is slow in getting angry, but when aroused, his power is incredible, and he does not easily forgive. He shows his power in the terrors of the cyclone and the raging storms; clouds are billowing dust beneath his feet! His fury is like fire. The mountains tumble down before his anger.

We cannot imagine the power of the Almighty, and yet he is so just and merciful that he does not destroy us. For Jehovah will vindicate his people, and have compassion on his servants.

Never avenge yourselves. Leave that to God, for he has said that he will repay those who deserve it. Conquer evil by doing good.

Psalm 94:1. Nahum 1:2, 3, 6. Job 37:23. Psalm 135:14. Romans 12:19, 21.

�∩AHUM

The Lord is good.

When trouble comes, he is the place to go! And he knows everyone who trusts in him!

... Live within the shadow of the Almighty, sheltered by the God who is above all gods. ... He will shield you with his wings! They will shelter you. His faithful promises are your armor.

Oh, love the Lord, all of you who are his people; for the Lord protects those who are loyal to him.

Jehovah God is our Light and our Protector. He gives us grace and glory. No good thing will he withhold from those who walk along his paths.

So also the Lord can rescue you and me from the temptations that surround us and continue to punish the ungodly until the day of final judgment comes.

Nahum 1:7. Psalm 91:1, 4. Psalm 31:23. Psalm 84:11. 2 Peter 2:9.

HABAKKUK

Have I been wasting my time?

O Lord, how long must I call for help before you will listen?

Wherever I look there is oppression and bribery and men who love to argue and to fight. The law is not enforced and there is no justice given in the courts for the wicked far outnumber the righteous, and bribes and trickery prevail.

Then one day I . . . thought about the future of these evil men. What a slippery path they are on—suddenly God will send them sliding over the edge of the cliff and down to their destruction: an instant end to all their happiness, an eternity of terror.

But those who trust the Lord shall be given every blessing. The Lord takes care of those he has forgiven.

Psalm 73:13. Habakkuk 1:2-4. Psalm 73:17-19. Psalm 37:9, 17.

HABAKKUK

You will be astounded at what I am about to do!

The time will come when all the earth is filled, as the waters fill the sea, with an awareness of the glory of the Lord.

The Lord said to me, ... "These things I plan won't happen right away. If it seems slow, do not despair, for these things will surely come to pass. Just be patient! They will not be overdue a single day!"

Don't be impatient. Wait for the Lord, and he will come and save you! Be brave, stouthearted and courageous. Yes, wait and he will help you.

But don't forget this, dear friends, that a day or a thousand years from now is like tomorrow to the Lord.

Habakkuk 1:5. Habakkuk 2:14, 2, 3. Psalm 27:14. 2 Peter 3:8.

HABAKKUK

The righteous man trusts in me, and lives!

This Good News tells us that God makes us ready for heaven—makes us right in God's sight—when we put our faith and trust in Christ to save us. This is accomplished from start to finish by faith. As the Scripture says it, "The man who finds life will find it through trusting God."

For God loved the world so much that he gave his only Son so that anyone who believes in him shall not perish but have eternal life. God did not send his Son into the world to condemn it, but to save it. There is no eternal doom awaiting those who trust him to save them.

Wicked men trust themselves alone . . . and fail.

Habakkuk 2:4. Romans 1:17. John 3:16-18. Habakkuk 2:4.

Even though the fig trees are all destroyed, and there is neither blossom left nor fruit, and though the olive crops all fail, and the fields lie barren; even if the flocks die in the fields and the cattle barns are empty, yet I will rejoice in the Lord. I will be happy in the God of my salvation. The Lord God is my Strength, and he will give me the speed of a deer and bring me safely over the mountains.

The Lord is my light and my salvation; whom shall I fear? When evil men come to destroy me, they will stumble and fall! Yes, though a mighty army marches against me, my heart shall know no fear! I am confident that God will save me.

I will trust and not be afraid, for the Lord is my strength and song; he is my salvation.

Habakkuk 3:3, 17-19. Psalm 27:1-3. Isaiah 12:2.

**His glory fills the heavens,
and the earth is full of his praise!
What a wonderful God he is!**

ZEPHANIAH

Subject: A message from the Lord.
To: Zephaniah

I will search with lanterns in Jerusalem's darkest corners to find and punish those who sit contented in their sins, indifferent to God, thinking he will let them alone.

Am I a God who is only in one place and cannot see what they are doing? Can anyone hide from me? Am I not everywhere in all of heaven and earth?

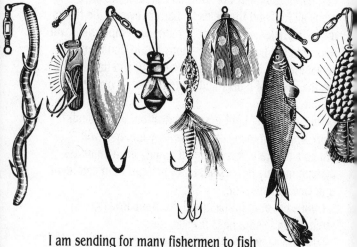

I am sending for many fishermen to fish you from the deeps where you are hiding from my wrath. I am sending for hunters to chase you down like deer in the forests or mountain goats on inaccessible crags. Wherever you run to escape my judgment, I will find you and punish you. For I am closely watching you and I see every sin. You cannot hope to hide from me.

Zephaniah 1:1, 12. Jeremiah 23:23, 24. Jeremiah 16:16, 17.

ZEPHANIAH

Walk humbly and do what is right.

If my people will humble themselves and pray, and search for me, and turn from their wicked ways, I will hear them from heaven and forgive their sins and heal their land. I will listen, wide awake, to every prayer made in this place.

The Lord is good and glad to teach the proper path to all who go astray; he will teach the ways that are right and best to those who humbly turn to him. And when we obey him, every path he guides us on is fragrant with his lovingkindness and his truth.

He has told you what he wants, and this is all it is: *to be fair and just and merciful and to walk humbly with your God.*

When you realize your worthlessness before the Lord, he will lift you up, encourage and help you.

Zephaniah 2:3. 2 Chronicles 7:14, 15. Psalm 25:8-10. Micah 6:8. James 4:10.

ZEPHANIAH

The Lord your God has arrived to live among you.

He is a mighty Savior. He will give you victory. He will rejoice over you in great gladness; he will love you and not accuse you.

He is able to save completely all who come to God through him. Since he will live forever, he will always be there to remind God that he has paid for their sins with his blood.

Rejoice greatly, O my people! Shout with joy! For look—your King is coming! He is the Righteous One, the Victor! Yet he is lowly, riding on a donkey's colt!

Arm yourself, O mighty one,
So glorious, so majestic!
And in your majesty
Go on to victory,
Defending truth, humility and justice.
Go forth to awe-inspiring deeds!

Zephaniah 3:17, 18. Hebrews 7:25. Zechariah 9:9. Psalm 45:3, 4.

**Don't
store up
treasures here on
earth where they can
erode away or may be stolen.**

Is it then the right time for you to live in
luxurious homes, when the Temple lies in
ruins? Don't think only of yourself.
Don't weary yourself trying to get rich. Why
waste your time? For riches can disappear as
though they had the wings of a bird. Better
poor and humble than proud and rich.
If you must choose, take a good name rather
than great riches; for to be held in loving
esteem is better than silver and gold.

Matthew 6:19. Haggai 1:3. 1 Corinthians 10:24.
Proverbs 23:4, 5. Proverbs 16:19. Proverbs 22:1.

HAGGAI

"Take courage . . .
for I am with you,"
says the Lord of Hosts.

Let us not get tired of doing what is right, for after a while we will reap a harvest of blessing if we don't get discouraged and give up.

When you put on a dinner . . . don't invite friends, brothers, relatives, and rich neighbors! Instead invite the poor, the crippled, the lame, and the blind.

When others are happy, be happy with them. If they are sad, share their sorrow.

Give what you have to anyone who asks you for it; and when things are taken away from you, don't worry about getting them back.

Haggai 2:4. Galatians 6:9. Luke 14:12, 13.
Romans 12:15. Luke 6:30.

HAGGAI

**Your own soul is nourished
when you are kind;
it is destroyed when you are
cruel.**

Living with selfish attitudes and evil hearts
... everything you did went wrong.

Don't just think about your own affairs,
but be interested in others, too, and in what
they are doing.

For people will love only themselves and
their money; they will be proud and
boastful, sneering at God, disobedient to
their parents, ungrateful to them, and
thoroughly bad. They will be hardheaded
and never give in to others; they will be
constant liars and troublemakers.

There will be no mercy to those who have
shown no mercy. But if you have been
merciful, then God's mercy toward you will
win out over his judgment against you.

Proverbs 11:17. Haggai 2:14, 15. Philippians 2:4.
2 Timothy 3:2, 3. James 2:13.

ZECHARIAH

**A Fountain
to cleanse
them from all
their sins
and uncleanness.**

For the Lamb standing in front of the throne will feed them and be their Shepherd and lead them to the springs of the Water of Life. And God will wipe their tears away.

They shall neither hunger nor thirst, the searing sun and scorching desert winds will not reach them any more. For the Lord in his mercy will lead them beside the cool waters. "The water I give them," (Jesus) said, "becomes a perpetual spring within them, watering them forever with eternal life."

Is anyone thirsty? Come and drink—even if you have no money!

Zechariah 13:1. Revelation 7:17.
Isaiah 49:10. John 4:14.
Isaiah 55:1.

ZECHARIAH

I have taken away your sins.

What happiness for those whose guilt has been forgiven! What joys when sins are covered over!

Your old life with all its wickedness . . . is dead and gone. You are living a brand new kind of life that is continually learning more and more of what is right, and trying constantly to be more and more like Christ who created this new life within you.

And when Christ who is our real life comes back again, you will shine with him and share in all his glories.

Zechariah 3:4. Psalm 32:1. Colossians 3:9, 10. Colossians 3:4.

ZECHARIAH

Shout with joy!
For look—
your King is coming!

He is the Righteous One, the Victor! Yet he is lowly, riding on a donkey's colt!

His realm shall stretch from sea to sea, from the river to the ends of the earth. Come to the place of safety, all you prisoners, for there is yet hope! I promise right now, I will repay you two mercies for each of your woes!

The Lord their God will save his people in that day, as a Shepherd caring for his sheep. They shall shine in his land as glittering jewels in a crown. How wonderful and beautiful all shall be! The abundance of grain and wine will make the young men and girls flourish; they will be radiant with health and happiness.

Zechariah 9:9, 10, 12, 16, 17.

MALACHI

They wouldn't listen; they kept on doing whatever they wanted to.

You don't honor me ... you despise my name. / *Who? Us? When?*

You offer polluted sacrifices on my altar. / *When have we ever done anything like that?*

You have wearied the Lord with your words. / *Wearied him? How have we wearied him?*

You have robbed me. / *What do you mean?*

Your attitude toward me has been proud and arrogant. / *What do you mean? What have we said that we shouldn't?*

Does not God have a perfect right to show his fury and power against those who are fit only for destruction, those he has been patient with for all this time?

Jeremiah 7:24. Malachi 1:6, 7. Malachi 2:17. Malachi 3:8, 13. Romans 9:22.

I am coming soon.

"Watch now," the Lord of Hosts declares, "the day of judgment is coming, burning like a furnace. The proud and wicked will be burned up like straw; like a tree, they will be consumed—roots and all.

"But for you who fear my name, the Sun of Righteousness will rise with healing in his wings. And you will go free, leaping with joy like calves let out to pasture. Then you will tread upon the wicked as ashes underfoot," says the Lord of Hosts.

Amen! Come, Lord Jesus!

Revelation 22:12. Malachi 4:1-3. Revelation 22:20.

MALACHI

Lift your eyes to see what God

Then you will say, "Truly, the Lord's great power goes far beyond our borders!"

He is the God who keeps every promise, and gives justice to the poor and oppressed, and food to the hungry. He frees the prisoners, and opens the eyes of the blind; he lifts the burdens from those bent down beneath their loads. For the Lord loves good men. He

is doing all around the world.

protects the immigrants, and cares for the orphans and
widows. But he turns topsy-turvy the plans of the
wicked.

The Lord will reign forever. O Jerusalem, your God is
King in every generation! Hallelujah! Praise the Lord!

Malachi 1:5. Psalm 146:6-10.

MALACHI

I am the Lord—I do not change.

"Though you have scorned my laws from earliest time, yet you may still return to me," says the Lord of Hosts. "Come and I will forgive you."

He is merciful and tender toward those who don't deserve it; he is slow to get angry and full of kindness and love. He never bears a grudge, nor remains angry forever. He has not punished us as we deserve for all our sins.

The Lord still waits for you to come to him so he can show you his love. For the Lord is faithful to his promises.

If we confess our sins to him, he can be depended on to forgive us and to cleanse us from every wrong.

Malachi 3:6, 7. Psalm 103:8-10. Isaiah 30:18. 1 John 1:9.

"I have loved you very deeply," says the Lord.

God is so rich in mercy, he loved us so much that even though we were spiritually dead and doomed by our sins, he gave us back our lives again when he raised Christ from the dead—only by his undeserved favor have we ever been saved.

He allows us to be called his children.

And he had a Book of Remembrance drawn up in which he recorded the names of those who feared him and loved to think about him.

"They shall be mine," says the Lord of Hosts, "in that day when I make up my jewels. And I will spare them as a man spares an obedient and dutiful son. Then you will see the difference between God's treatment of good men and bad, between those who serve him and those who don't."

Malachi 1:2, 3. Ephesians 2:4, 5. 1 John 3:1. Malachi 3:16-18.

MALACHI

**On every Lord's Day
each of you should put aside
something from what you
have earned during the week.**

"Bring all the tithes into the storehouse . . . if
you do, I will open up the windows of heaven
for you and pour out a blessing so great you
won't have room enough to take it in!

"Try it! Let me prove it to you! Your crops will
be large, for I will guard them from insects and
plagues. Your grapes won't shrivel away before
they ripen," says the Lord of Hosts. And all
nations will call you blessed, for you will be a
land sparkling with happiness. These are the
promises of the Lord of Hosts.

Remember this—if you give little, you will get
little.

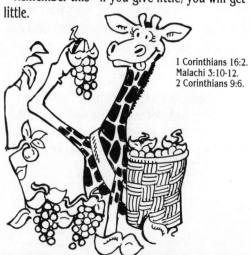

1 Corinthians 16:2.
Malachi 3:10-12.
2 Corinthians 9:6.

GOSPELS

Christ became a human being and lived here on earth among us.

My servant . . . my Chosen One, in whom I delight. I will put my Spirit upon him. He will reveal justice to the nations of the world.

He became flesh and blood . . . by being born in human form. For only as a human being could he die and in dying break the power of death.

All who trust him—God's Son—to save them have eternal life. Those who don't believe and obey him shall never see heaven, but the wrath of God remains upon them.

And the Lord shall be King over all the earth. In that day there shall be one Lord—his name alone will be worshiped.

John 1:14. Isaiah 42:1. Hebrews 2:14. John 3:36. Zechariah 14:9.

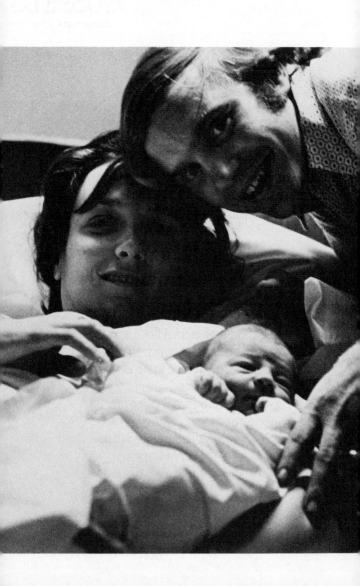

GOSPELS

Jesus Christ our Lord . . . came as a human baby.

Bethlehem . . . an unimportant Judean village . . . the birthplace of my King.

Mary . . . wrapped him in a blanket and laid him in a manger, because there was no room for them in the village inn.

You are to name him Jesus. He shall be very great and shall be called the Son of God. He shall be a King who shall rule with wisdom and justice and cause righteousness to prevail everywhere throughout the earth. At the name of Jesus every knee shall bow in heaven and on earth and under the earth, and every tongue shall confess that Jesus Christ is Lord, to the glory of God the Father.

Romans 1:3. Matthew 2:5. Luke 2:5-7. Luke 1:31, 32. Jeremiah 23:5, 6. Philippians 2:10, 11.

GOSPELS

The shepherds told everyone.

That night some shepherds were in the fields outside the village, guarding their flocks of sheep. Suddenly an angel appeared . . . "Don't be afraid!" he said. "I bring you the most joyful news ever announced and it is for everyone! The Savior . . . has been born tonight in Bethlehem!

They ran to the village. And there was the baby, lying in the manger. All who heard the shepherds' story expressed astonishment.

Sing to the Lord, for he has done wonderful things. Make known his praise around the world. Let all the people of Jerusalem shout his praise with joy.

Luke 2:17, 8-11, 16, 18. Isaiah 12:5, 6.

The astrologers . . . "We have seen his star . . . and have come to worship him."

Their joy knew no bounds! Entering the house where the baby and Mary his mother were, they threw themselves down before him, worshiping. Then they opened their presents and gave him gold, frankincense and myrrh.

Both proud and humble together, all who are mortal—born to die—shall worship him. All will bring their gifts. Yes, kings from everywhere! All will bow before him! All will serve him!

The people will proclaim, "This is our God, in whom we trust, for whom we waited. Now at last he is here." What a day of rejoicing!

Matthew 2:1, 2, 10, 11. Psalm 22:29.
Psalm 72:10, 11. Isaiah 25:9.

GOSPELS

King Herod is going to try to kill the child.

Not everyone who hears the Good News has welcomed it. For a summit conference of the nations has been called to plot against the Lord and his Messiah, Christ the King.

Herod was furious. Sending soldiers to Bethlehem, he ordered them to kill every baby boy two years old and under, both in the town and on the nearby farms. Joseph . . . left for Egypt with Mary and the baby, and stayed there until King Herod's death.

Even in his own land and among his own people, the Jews, he was not accepted. Only a few would welcome and receive him. But to all who received him, he gave the right to become children of God. All they needed to do was to trust him to save them.

Matthew 2:13. Romans 10:16. Psalm 2:2.
Matthew 2:16, 13-15. John 1:11, 12.

Jesus grew both tall and wise.

They . . . lived in Nazareth. There the child became a strong, robust lad, and was known for wisdom beyond his years.

. . . Sitting among the teachers of Law, discussing deep questions with them and amazing everyone with his understanding and answers. His parents didn't know what to think.

"How is this possible?" the people exclaimed. "He's just a carpenter's son."

You have given him fame and honor. You have clothed him with splendor and majesty. He will never stumble, never fall. For he depends upon the steadfast love of the God who is above all gods.

Luke 2:52. Matthew 2:23. Luke 2:40, 46-48. Matthew 13:55. Psalm 21:5, 7.

These will be his royal titles:

And the Spirit of the Lord shall rest upon him, the Spirit of wisdom, understanding, counsel and might; the Spirit of knowledge and of the fear of the Lord. His delight will be obedience to the Lord.

If you want to know what God wants you to do, ask him, and he will gladly tell you. For he is always ready to give a bountiful supply of wisdom to all who ask him. He will not resent it.

Put God first, and he will direct you and crown your efforts with success.

Isaiah 9:6. Isaiah 11:2, 3. James 1:5. Proverbs 3:6.

GOSPELS

These will be his royal titles:

You are the fairest of all. Your words are filled with grace. Arm yourself, O Mighty One, so glorious, so majestic! And in your majesty go on to victory, defending truth, humility and justice. Go forth to awe-inspiring deeds! Your throne, O God, endures forever. Justice is your royal scepter.

God's Son shines out with God's glory, and all that God's Son is and does marks him as God. He is the one who died to cleanse us and clear our record of all sin, and then sat down in highest honor beside the great God of Heaven.

Isaiah 9:6. Psalm 45:2-4, 6. Hebrews 1:3.

These will be his royal titles:

"I am the
A and the Z, the Beginning and the Ending of all things,"
says God, who is the Lord, the All Powerful One who is,
and was, and is coming again!

Of his Son he says, "Your kingdom, O God, will last
forever and ever."

God also called him "Lord" when he said, "Lord, in the
beginning you made the earth, and the heavens are the
work of your hands. They will disappear into
nothingness, but you will remain forever. They will
become worn out like old clothes, and some day you will
fold them up and replace them. But you yourself will
never change, and your years will never end."

In Christ there is all of God in a human body.

Isaiah 9:6. Revelation 1:8. Hebrews 1:8, 10-12. Colossians 2:9.

These will be his royal titles:

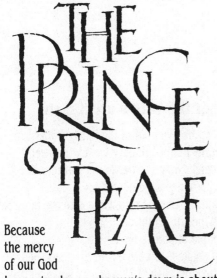

THE PRINCE OF PEACE

Because
the mercy
of our God
is very tender ... heaven's dawn is about to break upon
us, to give light to those who sit in darkness and death's
shadow, and to guide us to the path of peace.

Help him to give justice to your people, even to the
poor. May the mountains and hills flourish in prosperity
because of his good reign. Help him to defend the poor
and needy and to crush their oppressors.

God's peace ... far more wonderful than the human
mind can understand. His peace will keep your thoughts
and your hearts quiet and at rest as you trust in Christ
Jesus.

Isaiah 9:6. Luke 1:78, 79. Psalm 72:2-4. Philippians 4:7.

GOSPELS

John! One of the Lord's great men.

When he grew up he lived out in the lonely wilderness until he began his public ministry. His clothes were woven from camel's hair and he wore a leather belt. Locusts and wild honey were his food.

God sent John the Baptist as a witness to the fact that Jesus Christ is the true Light.

Here is a sample of John's preaching.

You brood of snakes! You are trying to escape hell without truly turning to God! That is why you want to be baptized! First go and prove by the way you live that you really have repented. If you have two coats . . . give one to the poor. If you have extra food, give it away to those who are hungry.

Luke 1:13, 15, 80. Mark 1:6. John 1:6, 7. Luke 3:7, 8, 11.

One day, after the crowds had been baptized, Jesus himself was baptized.

John didn't want to do it. "This isn't proper," he said. "I am the one who needs to be baptized by you."

But Jesus said, "Please do it, for I must do all that is right." So then John baptized him.

As soon as Jesus came up out of the water . . . a voice from heaven said, "This is my beloved Son, and I am wonderfully pleased with him."

In baptism you see how your old, evil nature died with him and was buried with him. And then you came up out of death with him into a new life because you trusted the Word of the mighty God who raised Christ from the dead.

Luke 3:21. Matthew 3:14-17. Colossians 2:12.

No temptation is irresistible.

For forty days and forty nights he (Jesus) ate nothing. Satan tempted him to get food by changing stones into loaves of bread. ☐ Jesus told him, "No! For the Scriptures tell us that bread won't feed men's souls: obedience to every word of God is what we need."

The roof of the Temple. "Jump off," he (Satan) said, "the Scriptures declare, 'God will send his angels to keep you from harm.' " ☐ Jesus retorted, "It also says not to put the Lord your God to a foolish test!"

The nations of the world. "I'll give it all to you . . . if you will only kneel and worship me." ☐ "Get out of here, Satan," Jesus told him. "The Scriptures say, 'Worship only the Lord God. Obey only him.' "

Those who love your laws have great peace of heart and mind and do not stumble.

1 Corinthians 10:13. Matthew 4:2-10. Psalm 119:165.

"Born again!" exclaimed Nicodemus. "What do you mean?"

After dark one night a Jewish religious leader named Nicodemus . . . came for an interview with Jesus. "Sir," he said, "we all know that God has sent you to teach us. Your miracles are proof enough of this."

Jesus replied, . . . "Unless you are born again, you can never get into the Kingdom of God. . . . Unless one

is born of water and the Spirit, he cannot enter the Kingdom of God. Men can only reproduce human life, but the Holy Spirit gives you new life from heaven, so don't be surprised at my statement that you must be born again!"

All those who believe this are reborn!

John 3:4, 1-3, 5-7. John 1:13.

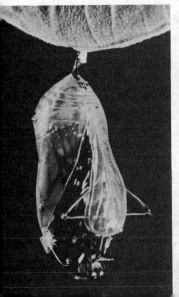

HUMBLE MEN ARE VERY FORTUNATE . . . FOR THE KINGDOM OF HEAVEN IS GIVEN TO THEM.

Are you seeking great things for yourself? Don't do it! Those who think themselves great shall be disappointed. He has told you what he wants, and this is all it is . . . to walk humbly with your God. All who humble themselves before the Lord shall be given every blessing, and shall have wonderful peace. The humble shall see their God at work for them. No wonder they will be so glad! All who seek for God shall live in joy.

Matthew 5:3. Jeremiah 45:5. Matthew 23:12. Micah 6:8. Psalm 37:11. Psalm 69:32.

THOSE WHO MOURN ARE FORTUNATE! FOR THEY SHALL BE COMFORTED.

What a
wonderful God
we have . . . who so wonderfully comforts and
strengthens us in our hardships and trials.

He is like a father to us, tender and sympathetic to
those who reverence him. He gives families to the lonely,
and releases prisoners from jail, singing with joy!

The young girls will dance for joy, and men folk—old
and young—will take their part in all the fun. For I will
turn their mourning into joy and I will comfort them and
make them rejoice.

Sing for joy, O heavens. Shout, O earth. Break forth
with a song, O mountains, for the Lord has comforted
his people, and will have compassion upon them in their
sorrow.

Matthew 5:4. 2 Corinthians 1:3. Psalm 103:13. Psalm 68:6. Jeremiah 31:13.
Isaiah 49:13.

GOSPELS

THE MEEK AND LOWLY ARE FORTUNATE . . .
FOR THE WHOLE WIDE WORLD BELONGS TO THEM.

Proud men
end in shame,
but the meek
become wise.

Be beautiful inside, in your hearts, with the lasting charm of a gentle and quiet spirit which is so precious to God.

Do you want a long, good life? Then watch your tongue! Keep your lips from lying. Turn from all known sin and spend your time in doing good. Try to live in peace with everyone. Work hard at it.

All who humble themselves before the Lord shall be given every blessing, and shall have wonderful peace.

Matthew 5:5. Proverbs 11:2. 1 Peter 3:4. Psalm 34:12-14. Psalm 37:11.

HAPPY ARE THOSE WHO LONG TO BE JUST AND GOOD, FOR THEY SHALL BE COMPLETELY SATISFIED.

Follow the steps of the godly . . . and stay on the right path. For only good men enjoy life to the full. Evil men lose the good things they might have had and they themselves shall be destroyed.

The man who tries to be good, loving and kind finds life, righteousness and honor. Live by the principles of love and justice, and always be expecting much from him, your God.

If you want a long and satisfying life, closely follow my instructions. Never forget to be truthful and kind. Hold these virtues tightly. Write them deep within your heart. They will lead you to real living.

Matthew 5:6. Proverbs 2:20-22. Proverbs 21:21. Hosea 12:6. Proverbs 3:2, 3. Proverbs 4:13.

GOSPELS

HAPPY ARE THE KIND AND MERCIFUL, FOR THEY SHALL BE SHOWN MERCY.

Love your enemies. Do good to those who hate you. Pray for the happiness of those who curse you. Implore God's blessing on those who hurt you. Then your reward from heaven will be very great, and you will truly be acting as sons of God. For he is kind to the unthankful and to those who are very wicked.

Try to show as much compassion as your Father does. Never criticize or condemn—or it will all come back on you. Go easy on others. Then they will do the same for you. When others are happy, be happy with them. If they are sad, share their sorrow.

Matthew 5:7. Luke 6:27, 28, 35-37. Romans 12:15.

HAPPY ARE THOSE WHOSE HEARTS ARE PURE, FOR THEY SHALL SEE GOD.

Who may climb the mountain of the Lord and enter where he lives? Who may stand before the Lord? Only those with pure hands and hearts, who do not practice dishonesty and lying. They will receive God's own goodness as their blessing from him, planted in their lives by God himself, their Savior.

Fix your thoughts on what is true and good and right. Think about things that are pure and lovely, and dwell on the fine, good things in others. Think about all you can praise God for and be glad about.

Stay close to anything that makes you want to do right. Have faith and love, and enjoy the companionship of those who love the Lord and have pure hearts.

Matthew 5:8, Psalm 24:3-5. Philippians 4:8. 2 Timothy 2:22.

HAPPY ARE THOSE WHO STRIVE FOR PEACE— THEY SHALL BE CALLED THE SONS OF GOD.

Don't get into needless fights. The Lord hates . . . sowing discord among brothers. Only fools insist on quarreling. If a brother sins against you, go to him privately and confront him with his fault. If he listens and confesses it, you have won back a brother. When a man is trying to please God, God makes even his worst enemies to be at peace with him. Those who are peacemakers will plant seeds of peace and reap a harvest of goodness. Most of all, let love guide your life.

Matthew 5:9. Proverbs 3:30. Proverbs 6:16. Proverbs 20:3. Matthew 18:15. Proverbs 16:7. James 3:18. Colossians 3:14.

Happy are those who are persecuted because they are good, for the Kingdom of Heaven is theirs.

Usually no one will hurt you for wanting to do good. But even if they should, you are to be envied. For God will reward you for it.

Do what is right. Then if men speak against you, calling you evil names, they will become ashamed of themselves for falsely accusing you when you have only done what is good. Remember, if God wants you to suffer, it is better to suffer for doing good than for doing wrong!

Christ also suffered. He died once for the sins of all us guilty sinners, although he himself was innocent of any sin at any time. Now Christ is in heaven, sitting in the place of honor next to God the Father, with all the angels and powers of heaven bowing before him and obeying him.

Matthew 5:10. 1 Peter 3:13, 14, 16-18, 22.

GOSPELS

You are the world's light.

—a city on a hill, glowing in the night for all to see. Don't hide your light! Let it shine for all.

No one lights a lamp and hides it! Instead he puts it on a lampstand to give light to all who enter the room.

Let your good deeds glow for all to see, so that they will praise your heavenly Father.

For though once your heart was full of darkness, now it is full of light from the Lord, and your behavior should show it! Because of this light within you, you should do only what is good and right and true.

Then you will become light bearers.

Matthew 5:14, 15. Luke 11:33. Matthew 5:16. Ephesians 5:8, 9. John 12:36.

GOSPELS

Take care! Don't do your good deeds publicly, to be admired.

For then you will lose the reward from your Father in heaven. When you give a gift to a beggar, don't shout about it.

But when you do a kindness to someone, do it secretly—don't tell your left hand what your right hand is doing. And your Father who knows all secrets will reward you.

And now about prayer. When you pray, don't be like the hypocrites who pretend piety by praying publicly . . . where everyone can see them. Truly, that is all the reward they will ever get.

But when you pray, go away by yourself, all alone, and shut the door behind you and pray to your Father secretly, and your Father, who knows your secrets will reward you.

Matthew 6:1-6.

Your Father knows exactly what you need.

Pray all the time. Ask God for anything in line with the Holy Spirit's wishes. Plead with him, reminding him of your needs. And keep praying earnestly for all Christians everywhere.

Pray along these lines:

OUR FATHER IN HEAVEN, WE HONOR YOUR HOLY NAME.

WE ASK THAT YOUR KINGDOM WILL COME NOW.

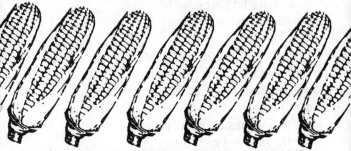

MAY YOUR WILL BE DONE HERE ON EARTH, JUST AS IT IS IN HEAVEN.

GIVE US OUR FOOD AGAIN TODAY, AS USUAL.

AND FORGIVE US OUR SINS, JUST AS WE HAVE FORGIVEN THOSE WHO HAVE SINNED AGAINST US.

DON'T BRING US INTO TEMPTATION, BUT DELIVER US FROM THE EVIL ONE. AMEN.

Matthew 6:8. Ephesians 6:18. Matthew 6:9-13.

GOSPELS

Our Father in heaven.

O Lord, you are our Father. We are the clay and you are the Potter. We are all formed by your hand.

There is only one God, the Father, who created all things and made us to be his own.

And so we should not be like cringing fearful slaves, but we should behave like God's very own children.

All of us ... may come to God the Father with the Holy Spirit's help because of what Christ has done for us.

What a wonderful God we have ... the source of every mercy, and the one who so wonderfully comforts and strengthens us in our hardships and trials.

Always give thanks for everything.

Matthew 6:9. Isaiah 64:8. 1 Corinthians 8:6.
Romans 8:15. Ephesians 2:18.
2 Corinthians 1:3. Ephesians 5:20.

Live one day at a time.

Don't worry about things—food, drink, and clothes.

Look at the birds! They don't worry about what to eat. They don't need to sow or reap or store up food—for your heavenly Father feeds them. And you are far more valuable to him than they are.

And why worry about your clothes? Look at the field lilies! They don't worry about theirs. Yet King Solomon in all his glory was not clothed as beautifully as they. And if God cares so wonderfully for flowers that are here today and gone tomorrow, won't he more surely care for you?

Your heavenly Father already knows perfectly well that you need them, and he will give them to you if you give him first place in your life and live as he wants you to.

Matthew 6:34, 25, 26, 28-30, 32, 33.

GOSPELS

Don't criticize, and then you won't be criticized.

For others will treat you as you treat them. Go easy on others; then they will do the same for you.

Stop being mean, bad-tempered and angry. Quarreling, harsh words, and dislike of others should have no place in your lives.

Dirty stories, foul talk and coarse jokes—these are not for you. Instead, remind each other of God's goodness and be thankful. Be done with dishonesty and jealousy and talking about others behind their backs.

Most important of all, continue to show deep love for each other, for love makes up for many of your faults.

Matthew 7:1, 2. Luke 6:37. Ephesians 4:31. Ephesians 5:4. 1 Peter 2:1. 1 Peter 4:8.

Treat others as you want them to treat you.

Don't repay evil for evil. Wait for the Lord to handle the matter.

To plan evil is as wrong as doing it. Do not rejoice when your enemy meets trouble. Let there be no gladness when he falls. Don't say, "Now I can pay him back for all his meanness to me!"

If someone slaps you on one cheek, let him slap the other too! If someone demands your coat, give him your shirt besides. Give what you have to anyone who asks you for it; and when things are taken away from you, don't worry about getting them back.

Try to show as much compassion as your Father does.

Luke 6:31. Proverbs 20:22.
Proverbs 24:8, 17, 29.
Luke 6:29, 30, 36.

GOSPELS

A fool thinks he needs no advice, but a wise man listens to others.

All who listen to my instructions and follow them are wise, like a man who builds his house on solid rock. Though the rain comes in torrents, and the floods rise and the storm winds beat against his house, it won't collapse, for it is built on rock.

But those who hear my instructions and ignore them are foolish, like a man who builds his house on sand. For when the rains and floods come, and storm winds beat against his house, it will fall with a mighty crash.

The advice of a wise man refreshes like water from a mountain spring. Those accepting it become aware of the pitfalls on ahead.

Proverbs 12:15. Matthew 7:24-27.
Proverbs 13:14.

GOSPELS

Whatever is in the heart overflows into speech.

A man's heart determines his speech. A good man's speech reveals the rich treasures within him. An evil-hearted man is filled with venom, and his speech reveals it.

The wicked accuse; the godly defend.

To quarrel with a neighbor is foolish; a man with good sense holds his tongue. A gossip goes around spreading rumors, while a trustworthy man tries to quiet them.

A fool is quick-tempered; a wise man stays cool when insulted. A good man is known by his truthfulness; a false man by deceit and lies. Some people like to make cutting remarks, but the words of the wise soothe and heal.

Luke 6:45. Matthew 12:34, 35. Proverbs 12:6. Proverbs 11:12, 13. Proverbs 12:16-18.

GOSPELS

**Was I too weak
to save you?
Have I no longer
power to deliver?
For I can
rebuke the sea
and make it dry!**

As evening fell, Jesus said to his disciples,
"Let's cross to the other side of the lake."

Then he got into a boat and started across
the lake. But soon a terrible storm arose. High
waves began to break into the boat until it was
nearly full of water and about to sink.

Jesus was asleep. The disciples went to him
and wakened him, shouting, "Lord, save us!
We're sinking!"

But Jesus answered, "O you men of little
faith! Why are you so frightened?" Then he
stood up and rebuked the wind and waves, and
the storm subsided and all was calm.

All that God's Son is and does marks him as
God. He regulates the universe by the mighty
power of his command.

Isaiah 50:2. Mark 4:35. Matthew 8:23. Mark 4:37.
Matthew 8:24-26. Hebrews 1:3.

GOSPELS

What is it that God has said?

Spend your energy seeking the eternal life that I, the Messiah, can give you. For God the Father has sent me for this very purpose.

My purpose is to give life in all its fullness. My sheep recognize my voice and I know them, and they follow me. I give them eternal life and they shall never perish. No one shall snatch them away from me.

It is he who saved us and chose us for his holy work, not because we deserved it but because that was his plan long before the world began—to show his love and kindness to us through Christ.

Master, to whom shall we go? You alone have the words that give eternal life, and we believe them and know you are the holy Son of God.

1 John 5:11. John 6:27. John 10:10, 27, 28. 2 Timothy 1:9. John 6:68, 69.

GOSPELS

It is the thought-life that pollutes.

For from within, out of men's hearts, come evil thoughts of lust, theft, murder, adultery, wanting what belongs to others, wickedness, deceit, lewdness, envy, slander, pride, and all other folly.

Your souls aren't harmed by what you eat, but by what you think and say!

You are controlled by your new nature if you have the Spirit of God living in you. And remember that if anyone doesn't have the Spirit of Christ living in him, he is not a Christian at all.

May my spoken words and unspoken thoughts be pleasing even to you, O Lord my Rock and my Redeemer. I will meditate about your glory, splendor, majesty, and miracles.

Mark 7:20-22, 15. Romans 8:9. Psalm 19:14. Psalm 145:5.

GOSPELS

Anyone wanting to be the greatest must be the least.

The more lowly your service to others, the greater you are. To be the greatest, be a servant. But those who think themselves great shall be disappointed and humbled; and those who humble themselves shall be exalted.

As you know, the kings and great men of the earth lord it over the people. But among you it is different. Whoever wants to be great among you must be your servant! For even I, the Messiah, am not here to be served, but to help others; and to give my life as a ransom for many.

People will come from all over the world to take their places there (in the Kingdom of God). And note this: some who are despised now will be greatly honored then. And some who are highly thought of now will be least important then.

Mark 9:35. Matthew 23:11, 12. Mark 10:42, 43, 45. Luke 13:29, 30.

Forgive anyone you are holding a grudge against.

Peter came to him (Jesus) and asked, "Sir, how often should I forgive a brother who sins against me? Seven times?"

"No!" Jesus replied, "seventy times seven!"

If someone mistreats you because you are a Christian, don't curse him; pray that God will bless him. Never pay back evil for evil. Do things in such a way that everyone can see you are honest clear through.

Be kind to each other, tenderhearted, forgiving one another, just as God has forgiven you because you belong to Christ.

Mark 11:25. Matthew 18:21, 22. Romans 12:14, 17. Ephesians 4:32.

GOSPELS

Why was this man born blind?

Was it a result of his own sins or those
of his parents?
"Neither," Jesus answered. "But to
demonstrate the power of God."
The Lord has anointed me to bring
good news to the suffering and
afflicted. He has sent me to comfort
the broken-hearted, to announce
liberty to captives and to open the
eyes of the blind.
Then Jesus told him, "I have come
into the world to give sight to those
who are spiritually blind and to show
those who think they see that they are
blind."
Who among you fears the Lord and
obeys his Servant? If such men walk in
darkness, without one ray of light, let
them trust the Lord, let them rely
upon their God.

John 9:2, 3. Isaiah 61:1. John 9:39. Isaiah 50:10.

GOSPELS

I am the Good Shepherd.
My purpose is to give life in all its fullness.

Because the Lord is my Shepherd, I have everything I need!

He lets me rest in the meadow grass and leads me beside the quiet streams. He restores my failing health. He helps me do what honors him the most.

Even when walking through the dark valley of earth I will not be afraid, for you are close beside me, guarding, guiding all the way.

You provide delicious food for me in the presence of my enemies. You have welcomed me as your guest. Blessings overflow!

Your goodness and unfailing kindness shall be with me all of my life, and afterwards I will live with you forever in your home.

John 10:11, 10. Psalm 23:1-6.

GOSPELS

**Where is the man
who fears the Lord?
God will teach him
how to choose the best.**

As Jesus and the disciples continued on their way to Jerusalem they came to a village where a woman named Martha welcomed them into her home. Her sister Mary sat on the floor, listening to Jesus as he talked.

But Martha was the jittery type, and was worrying over the big dinner she was preparing.

She came to Jesus and said, "Sir, doesn't it seem unfair to you that my sister just sits here while I do all the work? Tell her to come and help me."

But the Lord said to her, "Martha, dear friend, you are so upset over all these details! There is really only one thing worth being concerned about. Mary has discovered it—and I won't take it away from her!"

Be delighted with the Lord. Then he will give you all your heart's desires.

Psalm 25:12. Luke 10:38-42. Psalm 37:4.

GOSPELS

Why do you call me "Lord" when you won't obey me?

God loathes the gifts of evil men, especially if they are trying to bribe him!

They love to wear the robes of the rich and scholarly, and to have everyone bow to them as they walk through the markets. They love to sit in the best seats in the synagogues, and at the places of honor at banquets—but they shamelessly cheat widows out of their homes and then, to cover up the kind of men they really are, they pretend to be pious by praying long prayers in public. Because of this, their punishment will be the greater.

Such hypocrisy cannot be hidden forever. It will become as evident as yeast in dough.

Don't just pretend to be good! Be done with dishonesty and jealousy and talking about others behind their backs.

Luke 6:46. Proverbs 21:27. Mark 12:38-40. Luke 12:1, 2. 1 Peter 2:1.

GOSPELS

Every man is a fool who gets rich on earth but not in heaven.

Sell what you have and give to those in need. This will fatten your purses in heaven! And the purses of heaven have no rips or holes in them. Your treasures there will never disappear; no thief can steal them; no moth can destroy them. Wherever your treasure is, there your heart and thoughts will also be.

Real life and real living are not related to how rich we are.

Tell those who are rich not to be proud and not to trust in their money, which will soon be gone. But their pride and trust should be in the living God who always richly gives us all we need for our enjoyment. Tell them to use their money to do good. They . . . should give happily to those in need, always being ready to share with others whatever God has given them.

Luke 12:15, 21, 33, 34. 1 Timothy 6:17, 18.

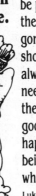

GOSPELS

Don't forget to be kind to strangers.

Some who have done this have entertained angels without realizing it!

When God's children are in need, you be the one to help them out. And get into the habit of inviting guests home for dinner or, if they need lodging, for the night.

When you put on a dinner . . . don't invite friends, brothers, relatives, and rich neighbors! For they will return the invitation. Instead, invite the poor, the crippled, the lame, and the blind. Then at the resurrection of the godly, God will reward you for inviting those who can't repay you.

Hebrews 13:2. Romans 12:13.
Luke 14: 12-14.

GOSPELS

Be just and fair to all, the Lord God says.

For unless you are honest in small matters, you won't be in large ones. If you cheat even a little, you won't be honest with greater responsibilities. And if you are untrustworthy about worldly wealth, who will trust you with the true riches of heaven? And if you are not faithful with other people's money, why should you be entrusted with money of your own?

Don't work hard only when your master is watching and then shirk when he isn't looking. Work hard and with gladness all the time. Blessings on you if I return and find you faithfully doing your work.

Isaiah 56:1. Luke 16:10-12. Ephesians 6:6. Matthew 24:46.

Do what's right and good.

GOSPELS

What I want from you is your true thanks.

Ten lepers stood at a distance, crying out, "Jesus, sir, have mercy on us!"

He looked at them and said, "Go to the Jewish priest and show him that you are healed!" And as they were going, their leprosy disappeared.

One of them came back to Jesus shouting, "Glory to God, I'm healed!" He fell flat on the ground in front of Jesus, face downward in the dust, thanking him for what he had done.

Jesus asked, "Didn't I heal ten men? Where are the nine?"

Always be thankful. Go home to your friends . . . and tell them what wonderful things God has done for you; and how merciful he has been.

Lord, I am overflowing with your blessings, just as you promised. Accept my grateful thanks and teach me your desires.

Psalm 50:14. Luke 17:12-17.
Colossians 3:15. Mark 5:19.
Psalm 119:65, 108.

GOSPELS

I . . . have come to search for and to save such souls as his.

When Jesus came by he looked up at Zacchaeus and called him by name!

"Zacchaeus!" he said. ". . . I am going to be a guest in your home today!"

Zacchaeus . . . took Jesus to his house in great excitement and joy.

But the crowds were displeased. "He has gone to be the guest of a notorious sinner," they grumbled.

Meanwhile, Zacchaeus stood before the Lord and said, "Sir, from now on I will give half my wealth to the poor, and if I find I have overcharged anyone on his taxes, I will penalize myself by giving him back four times as much!"

It is the sick who need a doctor, not those in good health. My purpose is to invite sinners to turn from their sins, not to spend my time with those who think themselves already good enough.

Luke 19:10, 5-8. Luke 5:31, 32.

GOSPELS

Good men will be generous to others and will be blessed of God for all they do.

As he (Jesus) stood in the Temple, he was watching the rich tossing their gifts into the collection box. Then a poor widow came by and dropped in two small copper coins.

"Really" he remarked, "this poor widow has given more than all the rest of them combined. For they have given a little of what they didn't need, but she, poor as she is, has given everything she has."

If you are really eager to give, then it isn't important how much you have to give. God wants you to give what you have, not what you haven't. God is able to make it up to you by giving you everything you need and more, so that there will not only be enough for your own needs, but plenty left over to give joyfully to others.

Isaiah 32:8. Luke 21:1-4. 2 Corinthians 8:12. 2 Corinthians 9:8.

Faith, hope, and love—and the greatest of these is love.

And so I (Jesus) am giving a new commandment to you now—love each other just as much as I love you. Your strong love for each other will prove to the world that you are my disciples.

Here is how to measure it—the greatest love is shown when a person lays down his life for his friends.

Love is very patient and kind, never jealous or envious, never boastful or proud, never haughty or selfish or rude. Love does not demand its own way. It is not irritable or touchy.

If you love someone you will be loyal to him no matter what the cost. You will always believe in him, always expect the best of him, and always stand your ground in defending him.

1 Corinthians 13:13. John 13:34, 35. John 15:13.
1 Corinthians 13:4, 5, 7.

GOSPELS

I will not abandon you or leave you as orphans in the storm — I will come to you.

If you love me, obey me. And I will ask the Father and he will give you another Comforter, and he will never leave you. He is the Holy Spirit, the Spirit who leads into all truth.

And when he has come he will convince the world of its sin, and of the availability of God's goodness, and of deliverance from judgment.

The world's sin is unbelief in me. There is righteousness available because I go to the Father.... There is deliverance from judgment because the prince of this world has already been judged.

When the Holy Spirit, who is truth, comes, he shall guide you into all truth. He shall praise me and bring me great honor by showing you my glory.

John 14:18, 15-17. John 16:8-11, 13, 14.

GOSPELS

The time has come!

Gathering the Twelve around him he (Christ) told them, "As you know, we are going to Jerusalem. And when we get there, all the predictions of the ancient prophets concerning me will come true. I, the Messiah, will be arrested and taken before the chief priests and the Jewish leaders, who will sentence me to die and hand me over to the Romans to be killed. They will mock me and spit on me and flog me with their whips and kill me. But after three days I will come back to life again."

He was willing to die a shameful death on the cross because of the joy he knew would be his afterwards. And now he sits in the place of honor by the throne of God.

Matthew 26:45. Luke 18:31.
Mark 10:33, 34. Hebrews 12:2.

GOSPELS

See, my Servant shall prosper; he shall be highly exalted.

Jesus went on towards Jerusalem.... He sent two disciples ahead ... to look for a donkey tied beside the road.... They brought the colt to Jesus and threw some of their clothing across its back for Jesus to sit on.

Then the crowds spread out their robes along the road ahead of him, and as they reached the place where the road started down from the Mount of Olives, the whole procession began to shout and sing as they walked along, praising God for all the wonderful miracles Jesus had done.

"God has given us a King!" they exulted. "Long live the King! Let all heaven rejoice! Glory to God in the highest heavens!"

Isaiah 52:13. Luke 19:28-30, 35-38.

GOSPELS

He . . . began to be filled with anguish and despair.

They sang a hymn and went out to the Mount of Olives. Jesus brought them to a garden grove, Gethsemane, and told them to sit down and wait while he went on ahead to pray.

He went forward a little, and fell face downward on the ground, and prayed, "My Father! If it is possible, let this cup be taken away from me. But I want your will, not mine."

Then an angel from heaven appeared and strengthened him, for he was in such agony of spirit that he broke into a sweat of blood, with great drops falling to the ground as he prayed more and more earnestly.

Matthew 26:37. Mark 14:26. Matthew 26:36, 39. Luke 22:43, 44.

This is your moment—the time when Satan's power reigns supreme!

Judas, the betrayer, knew this place, for Jesus had gone there many times with his disciples.

The chief priests and Pharisees had given Judas a squad of soldiers and police to accompany him. Now, with blazing torches, lanterns and weapons, they arrived at the olive grove.

Jesus fully realized all that was going to happen to him. Stepping forward to meet them he asked,

"Whom are you looking for?"

"Jesus of Nazareth," they replied.

"I am he," Jesus said.

He is the one who died to cleanse us and clear our record of all sin . . . who took God's wrath against our sins upon himself, and brought us into fellowship with God.

Then the mob arrested Jesus and held him fast.

Luke 22:53. John 18:2-5. Hebrews 1:3. 1 John 2:2. Mark 14:46.

GOSPELS

They demand that I be punished for what I didn't do.

Lord, how you have helped me before! You took me safely from my mother's womb and brought me through the years of infancy. I have depended upon you since birth; you have always been my God. Don't leave me now, for trouble is near and no one else can possibly help. O Lord, don't stay away. O God my Strength, hurry to my aid.

Save me, O my God. The floods have risen. Deeper and deeper I sink in the mire; the waters rise around me. I have wept until I am exhausted. My throat is dry and hoarse. My eyes are swollen with weeping, waiting for my God to act. I cannot even count all those who hate me without cause. They are influential men, these who plot to kill me though I am innocent.

Psalm 69:4. Psalm 22:9-11, 19. Psalm 69:1-4.

No one can kill me without my consent—I lay down my life voluntarily.

The mob led him to the home of Caiaphas the High Priest, where all the Jewish leaders were gathering.

The High Priest said to him, "I demand in the name of the living God that you tell us whether you claim to be the Messiah, the Son of God."

"Yes," Jesus said, "I am."

Then the High Priest tore at his clothing, shouting, "Blasphemy!... What is your verdict?"

They shouted,

DEATH!
DEATH!
DEATH!

The Jewish Supreme Court assembled ... took Jesus over to Pilate, the governor.

"We want him crucified," they demanded, "and your approval is required."

... So Pilate sentenced Jesus to die as they demanded.

John 10:18. Matthew 26:57, 63-66. Luke 22:66. Luke 23:1. John 18:31. Luke 23:24.

GOSPELS

He humbled himself . . . going so far as actually to die a criminal's death on a cross.

They had him at last, and he was taken out of the city, carrying his cross to the place known as "The Skull."

There they crucified him. . . . They sat around and watched him as he hung there.

"Father, forgive these people," Jesus said, "for they don't know what they are doing."

The people passing by hurled abuse, shaking their heads at him. And the chief priests and Jewish leaders also mocked him. "He saved others," they scoffed, "but he can't save himself!"

We are the ones who strayed away like sheep! *We,* who left God's paths to follow our own. Yet God laid on *him* the guilt and sins of every one of us!

Philippians 2:8. John 19:17, 18. Matthew 27:36. Luke 23:34.
Matthew 27:39, 41. Isaiah 53:6.

Everyone who sees me mocks and sneers and shrugs.

"Is this the one who rolled his burden on the Lord?" they laugh. "Is this the one who claims the Lord delights in him? We'll believe it when we see God rescue him!"

My strength has drained away like water, and all my bones are out of joint. My heart melts like wax. My strength has dried up like sunbaked clay. My tongue sticks to my mouth. The enemy, this gang of evil men, circles me like a pack of dogs; they have pierced my hands and feet.

You have let me sink down deep in desperate problems. But you will bring me back to life again, up from the depths of the earth.

Psalm 22:7, 8, 14-16. Psalm 71:20.

Jesus said, "When you have killed the Messiah, then you will realize that I am he."

That afternoon, the whole earth was covered with darkness for three hours, from noon until three o'clock.
Jesus knew that everything was now finished, and to fulfill the Scriptures said, "I'm thirsty." A jar of sour wine was sitting there, so a sponge was soaked in it and put

on a hyssop branch and held up to his lips. When Jesus had tasted it, he said, "It is finished."

Then Jesus shouted, "Father, I commit my spirit to you," and with those words he died.

When the captain of the Roman military unit handling the executions saw what had happened, he was stricken with awe before God and said, "Surely this man was innocent."

John 8:28. Matthew 27:45. John 19:28-30. Luke 23:46, 47.

GOSPELS

Early on Sunday morning ... Mary Magdalene and the other Mary went out to the tomb. When they arrived they looked up and saw that the stone—a very heavy one—was ... moved away and the entrance was open! So they went in—but the Lord Jesus' body was gone.

They stood there puzzled, trying to think what could have happened to it. Suddenly two men appeared before them, clothed in shining robes so bright their eyes were dazzled. The women were terrified and bowed low before them.

Then the men asked, "Why are you looking in a tomb for someone who is alive? He isn't here! He has come back to life again!

The women fled from the tomb, trembling and bewildered, too frightened to talk.

Acts 3:15. Matthew 28:1. Mark 16:4.
Luke 24:3-6. Mark 16:8.

God
brought
him back
to life
again.

GOSPELS

By being raised from the dead he was proved to be the mighty Son of God.

That evening the disciples were meeting behind locked doors ... when suddenly Jesus was standing there among them! How wonderful was their joy as they saw their Lord!

One of the disciples, Thomas, "The Twin," was not there at the time with the others. When they kept telling him, "We have seen the Lord," he replied, "I won't believe it unless I see the nail wounds in his hands—and put my fingers into them—and place my hand into his side."

Eight days later the disciples were together again, and this time Thomas was with them. The doors were locked; but suddenly, as before, Jesus was standing among them and greeting them. Then he said to Thomas, "Don't be faithless any longer. Believe!"

"My Lord and my God!" Thomas said.

Romans 1:4. John 20:19, 20, 24-28.

GOSPELS

There are many homes up there where my Father lives, and I am going to prepare them for your coming. When everything is ready, then I will come and get you, so that you can always be with me where I am. If this weren't so, I would tell you plainly. No, I will not abandon you or leave you as orphans in the storm—I will come to you.

It was not long afterwards that he rose into the sky and disappeared into a cloud, leaving them staring after him.

John 14:19, 2, 3, 18. Acts 1:9.

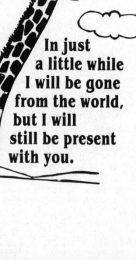

In just a little while I will be gone from the world, but I will still be present with you.

GOSPELS

Sing a new song to the Lord!

Sing it everywhere around the world!
Sing out his praises! Bless his name.
Each day tell someone that he saves.
Publish his glorious acts throughout
the earth. Tell everyone about the
amazing things he does. For the Lord
is great beyond description, and
greatly to be praised.

Jesus' disciples saw him do many
other miracles besides the ones told
about in this book, but these are
recorded so that you will believe that
he is the Messiah, the Son of God, and
that believing in him, you will have
life.

And I suppose that if all the other
events in Jesus' life were written, the
whole world could hardly contain the
books!

Psalm 96:1-4. John 20:30, 31. John 21:25.

GOSPELS

O God, in mercy bless us; let your face beam with joy as you look down at us.

Send us around the world with the news of your saving power and your eternal plan for all mankind. How everyone throughout the earth will praise the Lord! How glad the nations will be, singing for joy because you are their King and will give true justice to their people!

Praise God, O world! May all the peoples of the earth give thanks to you. For the earth has yielded abundant harvests. God, even our own God, will bless us. And peoples from remotest lands will worship him.

Psalm 67:1-7.

acts

I will pour out my Holy Spirit upon all mankind.

As the believers met together ... suddenly there was a sound like the roaring of a mighty windstorm in the skies above them and it filled the house where they were meeting. And everyone present was filled with the Holy Spirit and began speaking in languages they didn't know, for the Holy Spirit gave them this ability.

Peter stepped forward with the eleven apostles, and shouted to the crowd, ... "Each one of you must turn from sin, return to God, and be baptized in the name of Jesus Christ for the forgiveness of your sins. Then you also shall receive this gift, the Holy Spirit. For Christ promised him to each one of you who has been called by the Lord our God."

Acts 2:17, 1, 2, 4, 14, 38, 39.

acts

Peter preached a long sermon, telling about Jesus and strongly urging all his listeners to save themselves from the evils of their nation.

And those who believed Peter were baptized—about 3,000 in all! They joined with the other believers in regular attendance at the apostles' teaching sessions and at the Communion services and prayer meetings.

And all the believers met together constantly and shared everything with each other, selling their possessions and dividing with those in need. They worshiped together regularly at the Temple each day, met in small groups in homes for Communion, and shared their meals with great joy and thankfulness, praising God.

The whole city was favorable to them.

Acts 2:47,40-42,44-47.

acts

Everyone stood there awed by the wonderful thing that had happened.

As Peter and John approached the Temple, they saw a man lame from birth carried along the street, and laid beside the Temple gate . . . as was his custom every day.

Peter said, "We don't have any money for you! But I'll give you something else! I command you in the name of Jesus Christ of Nazareth, *walk!*

He came up with a leap, stood there a moment and began walking! Then, walking, leaping and praising God, he went into the Temple with them.

Peter saw his opportunity and addressed the crowd. "What is so surprising about this? Faith in Jesus' name—faith given us from God—has caused this perfect healing.

"Now change your mind and attitude to God and turn to him so he can cleanse away your sins."

Acts 3:11,1,2,6,8,12,16,19.

All the believers were of one heart and mind.

No one felt that what he owned was his own; everyone was sharing.

The apostles preached powerful sermons about the resurrection of the Lord Jesus, and there was warm fellowship among all the believers, and no poverty—for all who owned land or houses sold them and brought the money to the apostles to give to others in need.

Joseph . . . was one of those who sold a field he owned and brought the money to the apostles for distribution to those in need.

If God has given you money, be generous in helping others with it.

Acts 4:32-37. Romans 12:8.

acts

When we lie to each other we are hurting ourselves.

There was a man named Ananias (with his wife Sapphira) who sold some property, and brought only part of the money, claiming it was the full price.

But Peter said, "Ananias, Satan has filled your heart. When you claimed this was the full price, you were lying to the Holy Spirit. The property was yours to sell or not, as you wished. And after selling it, it was yours to decide how much to give. How could you do a thing like this? You weren't lying to us, but to God."

As soon as Ananias heard these words, he fell to the floor, dead! About three hours later his wife came in. . . . Instantly she fell to the floor, dead!

Terror gripped the entire church and all others who heard what had happened.

Don't swear that something is true when it isn't! To be held in loving esteem is better than silver and gold.

Ephesians 4:25. Acts 5:1-5, 7, 10, 11.
Zechariah 8:17. Ecclesiastes 7:1.

acts

The only thing we know about these Christians is that they are denounced everywhere!

The believers who had fled Jerusalem went everywhere preaching the Good News about Jesus!

Everything that has happened . . . has been a great boost in getting out the Good News concerning Christ. God turned into good what you meant for evil.

Yes, we live under constant danger to our lives because we serve the Lord, but this gives us constant opportunities to show forth the power of Jesus Christ within our dying bodies. Because of our preaching we face death, but it has resulted in eternal life for you.

Acts 5:41. Acts 28:22. Acts 8:4. Philippians 1:12. Genesis 50:20. 2 Corinthians 4:11, 12.

God had counted them worthy to suffer dishonor for his name.

acts

How patient he is with even the worst sinners.

I (Paul) used to believe that I ought to do many horrible things to the followers of Jesus of Nazareth. I used torture to try to make Christians everywhere curse Christ.

I was on such a mission to Damascus . . . a light from heaven brighter than the sun shone down on me . . . I heard a voice . . . "Saul, Saul, why are you persecuting me? You are only hurting yourself. I am Jesus, the one you are persecuting. Now stand up! For I have appeared to you to appoint you as my servant and my witness."

Whatever I am now it is all because God poured out such kindness and grace upon me. For even before I was born God had chosen me to be his.

1 Timothy 1:16. Acts 26:9, 11-16. 1 Corinthians 15:10. Galatians 1:15.

acts

I (Paul) have done the Lord's work humbly— yes, and with tears.

I have had one message for Jews and Gentiles alike—the necessity of turning from sin to God through faith in our Lord Jesus Christ.

The Holy Spirit has told me in city after city that jail and suffering lie ahead. But life is worth nothing unless I use it for doing the work assigned me by the Lord Jesus—the work of telling others the Good News about God's mighty kindness and love.

I am ready not only to be jailed at Jerusalem, but also to die for the sake of the Lord Jesus.

Only those who throw away their lives for my sake and for the sake of the Good News will ever know what it means to really live.

Acts 20:19, 21, 23, 24. Acts 21:13. Mark 8:35.

ROMANS

**All
have
sinned.
All
fall short
of God's
glorious ideal.**

As the Scriptures say, No one is good—no one in all the world is innocent. The heart is the most deceitful thing there is, and desperately wicked. No one can really know how bad it is!

I really want to do what is right, but I can't. I do what I don't want to, what I hate. When I want to do good, I don't. And when I try not to do wrong, I do it anyway.

Come, let's talk this over, says the Lord. No matter how deep the stain of your sins, I can take it out and make you as clean as freshly fallen snow. Even if you are stained as red as crimson, I can make you white as wool!

Romans 3:23. Romans 3:10. Jeremiah 17:9. Romans 7:15, 19. Isaiah 1:18.

God declares us

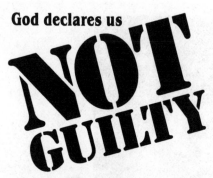

NOT GUILTY

**of offending him
if we trust in Jesus Christ.**

. . . Who in his kindness freely takes away our sins.

For God sent Christ Jesus to take the punishment for our sins and to end all God's anger against us.

And we all can be saved in this same way, by coming to Christ, no matter who we are or what we have been like.

Salvation that comes from trusting Christ . . . is already within easy reach of us; in fact it is as near as our own hearts and mouths.

For if you tell others with your own mouth that Jesus Christ is your Lord, and believe in your own heart that God has raised him from the dead, you will be saved.

Romans 3:24, 25, 22. Romans 10:8, 9.

ROMANS

We are saved by faith in Christ and not by the good things we do.

It is he who saved us and chose us for his holy work, not because we deserved it but because that was his plan long before the world began.

Because of his kindness you have been saved through trusting Christ. And even trusting is not of yourselves; it too is a gift from God. Salvation is not a reward for the good we have done, so none of us can take any credit for it.

The fact of the matter is this: when we try to gain God's blessing and salvation by keeping his laws we always end up under his anger, for we always fail to keep them.

Does this mean that we no longer need obey God's laws? Just the opposite! In fact, only when we trust Jesus can we truly obey him.

Romans 3:28. 2 Timothy 1:9. Ephesians 2:8, 9. Romans 4:15. Romans 3:31.

ROMANS

No one who believes in Christ will ever be disappointed.

He personally carried the load of our sins in his own body when he died on the cross, so that we can be finished with sin and live a good life from now on. For his wounds have healed ours!

What can we ever say to such wonderful things as these? If God is on our side, who can ever be against us? Since he did not spare even his own Son for us but gave him up for us all, won't he also surely give us everything else?

He will give you, through his great power, everything you need for living a truly good life; he even shares his own glory and his own goodness with us!

Romans 10:11. 1 Peter 2:24. Romans 8:31, 32. 2 Peter 1:3.

ROMANS

Since we have been made right in God's sight by faith in his promises, we can have real peace with him because of what Jesus Christ our Lord has done for us. For because of our faith, he has brought us into this place of highest privilege where we now stand, and we confidently and joyfully look forward to actually becoming all that God has had in mind for us to be.

We can rejoice, too, when we run into problems and trials for we know that they are good for us—they help us learn to be patient.

And patience develops strength of character in us and helps us trust God more each time we use it until finally our hope and faith are strong and steady.

Psalm 32:2. Romans 5:1-4.

What relief for those who have confessed their sins and God has cleared their record.

ROMANS

Now you can really serve God.

Not in the old way, mechanically obeying a set of rules, but in the new way—with all of your hearts and minds.

Give your bodies to God. Let them be a living sacrifice, holy—the kind he can accept. When you think of what he has done for you, is this too much to ask?

Don't copy the behavior and customs of this world, but be a new and different person with a fresh newness in all you do and think. Then you will learn from your own experience how his ways will really satisfy you.

For everything comes from God alone. Everything lives by his power, and everything is for his glory. To him be glory evermore.

Romans 7:6. Romans 12:1, 2. Romans 11:36.

1 Corinthians

Let *Love* be your greatest aim.

If I had the gift of being able to speak in other languages without learning them, and could speak in every language there is in all of heaven and earth, but didn't love others, I would only be making noise.

If I had the gift of prophecy and knew all about what is going to happen in the future, knew everything about everything, but didn't love others, what good would it do?

Even if I had the gift of faith so that I could speak to a mountain and make it move, I would still be worth nothing at all without love.

If I gave everything I have to poor people, and if I were burned alive for preaching the Gospel but didn't love others, it would be of no value whatever.

Don't just pretend that you love others; really love them.

1 Corinthians 14:1.
1 Corinthians 13:1-3.
Romans 12:9.

1 Corinthians

**Happy is the man
who has the God of Jacob
as his helper,
whose hope is
in the Lord his God.**

No mere man has ever seen, heard or even
imagined what wonderful things God has ready
for those who love the Lord.
God will shed his own glorious light upon
you. He will heal you. Your godliness will lead
you forward. Goodness will be a shield before
you. The glory of the Lord will protect you from behind.
Feed the hungry! Help those in trouble! Then
your light will shine out from the darkness and
the darkness around you shall be as bright as day.
And the Lord will guide you continually, and
satisfy you with all good things, and keep you
healthy too. And you will be like a well-watered
garden, like an everflowing spring.

Psalm 146:5. 1 Corinthians 2:9. Isaiah 58:8, 10, 11.

1 Corinthians

Do everything for the glory of God.

Keep your eyes open for spiritual danger. Stand true to the Lord. Act like men. Be strong. And whatever you do, do it with kindness and love.

I want you always to see clearly the difference between right and wrong, and to be inwardly clean, no one being able to criticize you from now until our Lord returns. May you always be doing those good, kind things which show that you are a child of God, for this will bring much praise and glory to the Lord.

Jesus . . . stood a little child beside him and said, " . . . Anyone who takes care of a little child like this is caring for me! And whoever cares for me is caring for God who sent me. Your care for others is the measure of your greatness."

1 Corinthians 10:31. 1 Corinthians 16:13. Philippians 1:10, 11. Luke 9:47, 48.

1 Corinthians

Few of you who follow Christ have big names or power or wealth.

Instead God has deliberately chosen to use ideas the world considers foolish and of little worth in order to shame those people considered by the world as wise and great. So that no one anywhere can ever brag in the presence of God.

So what about these wise men, these scholars, these brilliant debaters of this world's great affairs? God has made them all look foolish, and shown their wisdom to be useless nonsense. For God in his wisdom saw to it that the world would never find God through human brilliance. Then he stepped in and saved all those who believed his message, which the world calls foolish and silly.

Christ is the mighty power of God to save them; Christ himself is the center of God's wise plan for their salvation.

1 Corinthians 1:26, 27, 29, 20, 21, 24.

1 Corinthians

How will the dead be brought back to life again? What kind of bodies will they have?

You will find the answer in your own garden! When you put a seed into the ground it doesn't grow into a plant unless it dies first. And when the green shoot comes up out of the seed, it is very different from the seed you first planted.

For all you put into the ground is a dry little seed of wheat, or whatever it is you are planting, then God gives it a beautiful new body—just the kind he wants it to have.

Our earthly bodies which die and decay are different from the bodies we shall have when we come back to life again, for they will never die.

Since future victory is sure, be strong and steady, always abounding in the Lord's work.

1 Corinthians 15:35-38, 42, 58.

2 Corinthians

Power and success comes from God.

When I am weak, then I am strong—the less I have,
the more I depend on him.
I pray that you will begin to understand how incredibly
great his power is to help those who believe him.
Even strong, young lions sometimes go hungry, but
those of us who reverence the Lord will never lack any
good thing.
In the farthest corners of the earth the glorious acts of
God shall startle everyone. The dawn and sunset shout
for joy! He waters the earth to make it fertile. The rivers
of God will not run dry! He prepares the earth for his
people and sends them rich harvests of grain. He waters
the furrows with abundant rain.
Showers soften the earth, melting the
clods and causing seeds to sprout across the
land. Then he crowns it all with green, lush
pastures in the wilderness; hillsides
blossom with joy.

2 Corinthians 3:5.   2 Corinthians 12:10.
Psalm 34:10.   Psalm 65:8-12.

2 Corinthians

We are Christ's ambassadors. In everything you do, stay away from complaining and arguing, so that no one can speak a word of blame against you.

You are to live clean innocent lives as children of God in a dark world full of people who are crooked and stubborn. Shine out among them like beacon lights, holding out to them the Word of Life.

Don't let anyone think little of you because you are young. Be their ideal; let them follow the way you teach and live; be a pattern for them in your love, your faith, and your clean thoughts.

2 Corinthians 3:18. 2 Corinthians 5:20. Philippians 2:14-16.
1 Timothy 4:12.

We can be mirrors that brightly reflect the glory of the Lord.

2 Corinthians

Don't be teamed with those who do not love the Lord.

For what do the people of
God have in common with the people
of sin? How can light live with
darkness? And what harmony can
there be between Christ and the devil?
How can a Christian be a partner with
one who doesn't believe?

Oh, the joys of those who do not
follow evil men's advice, who do not
hang around with sinners, scoffing at
the things of God. But they delight in
doing everything God wants them to,
and day and night are always
meditating on his laws and thinking
about ways to follow him more closely.

They are like trees along a river
bank bearing luscious fruit each
season without fail. Their leaves shall
never wither, and all they do shall
prosper.

2 Corinthians 6:14, 15. Psalm 1:1-3.

2 Corinthians

God cheers those who are discouraged.

Here on earth you will have many trials and sorrows: but cheer up, for I have overcome the world.

You can be sure that the more we undergo sufferings for Christ, the more he will shower us with his comfort and encouragement.

And why does he do this? So that when others are troubled, needing our sympathy and encouragement, we can pass on to them this same help and comfort God has given us.

All who are oppressed may come to him. He is a refuge for them in their times of trouble. All those who know your mercy, Lord, will count on you for help. For you have never yet forsaken those who trust in you.

2 Corinthians 7:6. John 16:33. 2 Corinthians 1:5, 4. Psalm 9:9, 10.

GALATIANS

Jesus told him,
**"I am the Way—
yes, and the Truth
and the Life.
No one can get
to the Father
except
by means of me."**

Eternal life is in him,
and this life gives light
to all mankind.

If you believe that Jesus is the Christ—that he is God's Son and your Savior—then you are a child of God.

What is it that God has said? That he has given us eternal life, and that this life is in his Son. So whoever has God's Son has life; whoever does not have his Son, does not have life.

I have written this to you who believe in the Son of God so that you may know you have eternal life.

John 14:6. John 1:4. 1 John 5:1, 11-13.

GALATIANS

How different from the way of faith is the way of law which says that a man is saved by obeying every law of God, without one slip. But Christ has brought us out from under the doom of that impossible system by taking the curse for our wrongdoing upon himself. You know how full of love and kindness our Lord Jesus Christ was. Though he was so very rich, yet to help you he became so very poor, so that by being poor he could make you rich. He died for our sins just as God our Father planned, and rescued us from this evil world in which we live.

Galatians 3:11-13. 2 Corinthians 8:9. Galatians 1:45.

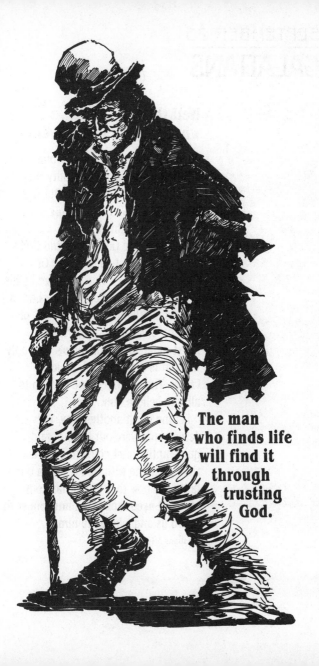

The man who finds life will find it through trusting God.

GALATIANS

Well then, why were the laws given?

They were added after the promise was given, to show men how guilty they are of breaking God's laws. But this system of law was to last only until the coming of Christ.

Well then, are God's laws and God's promises against each other? Of course not! If we could be saved by his laws, then God would not have had to give us a different way to get out of the grip of sin—for the Scriptures insist we are all its prisoners. The only way out is through faith in Jesus Christ. The way of escape is open to all who believe him.

Let me put it another way. The Jewish laws were our teacher and guide until Christ came to give us right standing with God through our faith. But now that Christ has come, we don't need those laws any longer to guard us and lead us to him.

Galatians 3:19, 21, 22, 24, 25.

What counts is whether we really have been changed into new and different people.

When someone becomes a Christian he becomes a brand new person inside. He is not the same anymore. A new life has begun! All these new things are from God who brought us back to himself through what Christ Jesus did.

Learn to know God better and discover what he wants you to do. Next, learn to put aside your own desires so that you will become patient and godly, gladly letting God have his way with you.

This will make possible the next step, which is for you to enjoy other people and to like them, and finally you will grow to love them deeply. The more you go on in this way, the more you will grow spiritually and become fruitful and useful to our Lord Jesus Christ.

Galatians 6:15. 2 Corinthians 5:17, 18. 2 Peter 1:5-8.

GALATIANS

**You have been given freedom:
not freedom to do wrong,
but freedom to love and serve each other.**

For the whole Law can be summed up in this one
command: Love others as you love yourself. But if
instead of showing love among yourselves you are
always critical and catty, watch out! Beware of ruining
each other.

   Don't just pretend that you love others: really love
them. Hate what is wrong. Stand on the side of the good.
Love each other with brotherly affection and take
delight in honoring each other. Never be lazy in your
work but serve the Lord enthusiastically.

Galatians 5:13-15. Romans 12:9-11.

GALATIANS

**Let us follow
the Holy Spirit's leading
in every part of our lives.**

When you follow your own wrong
inclinations your lives will produce
these evil results:

hatred and fighting,
  jealousy and anger,
    constant effort to get the best for
    yourself,
      complaints and criticisms,
        the feeling that everyone else is wrong
          except those in your own little
          group.

  But when the Holy Spirit controls
our lives he will produce this kind of
fruit in us:

love,
  joy,
    peace,
      patience,
        kindness,
          goodness,
            faithfulness,
              gentleness and
                self-control.

Galatians 5:25, 19, 20, 22, 23.

GALATIANS

Those false teachers who are so anxious to win your favor are not doing it for your good.

Stay away from those who cause divisions and are upsetting people's faith, teaching things about Christ that are contrary to what you have been taught. Such teachers are not working for our Lord Jesus, but only want gain for themselves. They are good speakers, and simple-minded people are often fooled by them.

For there is going to come a time when people won't listen to the truth, but will go around looking for teachers who will tell them just what they want to hear.

False teachers ... come disguised as harmless sheep, but are wolves and will tear you apart.

Galatians 4:17. Romans 16:17, 18. 2 Timothy 4:3. Matthew 7:15.

EPHESIANS

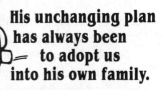

**His unchanging plan
has always been
to adopt us
into his own family.**

To all who received him, he gave the right to become children of God. All they needed to do was to trust him to save them.

And since we are his children, we will share his treasures—for all God gives to his Son Jesus is now ours too.

See how very much our heavenly Father loves us, for he allows us to be called his children—think of it—and we really are!

And so we should not be like cringing, fearful slaves, but we should behave like God's very own children, adopted into the bosom of his family, and calling to him, "Father, Father."

Ephesians 1:5. John 1:12. Romans 8:17.
1 John 3:1. Romans 8:15.

THE FUTURE HE HAS CALLED

For the good man—the blameless, the upright, the man of peace—he has a wonderful future ahead of him. For him there is a happy ending.

Be delighted with the Lord. Then he will give you all your heart's desires. Commit everything you do to the Lord. Trust him to help you do it and he will.

Keep traveling steadily along his pathway and in due

YOU TO SHARE.

season he will honor you with every blessing.

For the eyes of the Lord search back and forth across the whole earth, looking for people whose hearts are perfect toward him, so that he can show his great power in helping them.

Ephesians 1:18. Psalm 37:37, 4, 34. 2 Chronicles 16:9.

EPHESIANS

**How well he understands us
and knows what is best
for us at all times.**

True wisdom and power are God's. He
alone knows what we should do; he
understands.

He does whatever he thinks best
among the hosts of heaven, as well as
here among the inhabitants of earth.
No one can stop him or challenge him,
saying, "What do you mean by doing
these things?"

What a God he is! How perfect in
every way! All his promises prove true.
He is a shield for everyone who hides
behind him.

And when we obey him, every path
he guides us on is fragrant with his
lovingkindness and his truth.

Ephesians 1:8. Job 12:13. Daniel 4:35. Psalm
18:30. Psalm 25:10.

We can come fearlessly right into God's presence.

He is close to all who call on him sincerely. He fulfills the desires of those who reverence and trust him; he hears their cries for help and rescues them.

Out of his glorious, unlimited resources he will give you the mighty inner strengthening of his Holy Spirit. And I pray that Christ will be more and more at home in your hearts, living within you as you trust in him. May your roots go down deep into the soil of God's marvelous love. And may you be able to feel and understand as all God's children should, how long, how wide, how deep, and how high his love really is; and to experience this love for yourselves, though it is so great that you will never see the end of it or fully know or understand it.

Ephesians 3:12. Psalm 145:18, 19. Ephesians 3:16-19.

Be careful how you act.

Don't be fools; be wise. Make the most of every opportunity you have for doing good. Don't act thoughtlessly, but try to find out and do whatever the Lord wants you to.

All who listen to my instructions and follow them are wise, like a man who builds his house on solid rock. Though the rain comes in torrents, and the floods rise and the storm winds beat against his house, it won't collapse, for it is built on rock.

Guard my words as your most precious possession. Write them down, and also keep them deep within your heart.

Ephesians 5:15-17. Matthew 7:24, 25.
Proverbs 7:2, 3.

EPHESIANS

Live no longer as the unsaved do.

That isn't the way Christ taught you! Your attitudes and thoughts must all be constantly changing for the better.

☐ Stop lying to each other; tell the truth ... when we lie to each other we are hurting ourselves.

☐ If you are angry, don't sin by nursing your grudge. Don't let the sun go down with you still angry—get over it quickly. For when you are angry you give a mighty foothold to the devil.

☐ If anyone is stealing he must stop it.

☐ Don't use bad language. Say only what is helpful and good.

Be kind to each other, tender-hearted, forgiving one another, just as God has forgiven you because you belong to Christ.

Ephesians 4:17, 20, 23, 25-29, 32.

EPHESIANS

Obey your parents.

This is the right thing to do because God has placed them in authority over you. Honor your father and mother. This is the first of God's Ten Commandments that ends with a promise. And this is the promise: that if you honor your father and mother, yours will be a long life, full of blessing.

Tie their instructions around your finger so you won't forget. Take to heart all of their advice. Every day and all night long their counsel will lead you and save you from harm. When you wake up in the morning, let their instructions guide you into the new day. For their advice is a beam of light directed into the dark corners of your mind to warn you of danger and to give you a good life.

Ephesians 6:1-3. Proverbs 6:20-23.

PHILIPPIANS

Always be full of joy in the Lord.

Rejoice before the Lord your God in everything you do.
Majesty and honor march before him, strength and
gladness walk beside him.

Happy are all who perfectly follow the laws of God.
Happy are all who search for God, and always do his will.
I have recited your laws, and rejoiced in them more than
in riches. I will delight in them and not forget them. I
obey them even at night and keep my thoughts, O Lord,
on you. Your laws are my joyous treasure forever. I
rejoice in your laws like one who finds a great treasure.

Philippians 4:4. Deuteronomy 12:18. 1 Chronicles 16:27. Psalm 119:1, 2,
13, 14, 16, 55, 111, 162.

PHILIPPIANS

Remember always to live as Christians should.

... Careful to do the good things that result from being saved, obeying God with deep reverence, shrinking back from all that might displease him. For God is at work within you, helping you want to obey him, and then helping you do what he wants.

In everything you do, stay away from complaining and arguing, so that no one can speak a word of blame against you. You are to live clean, innocent lives as children of God in a dark world full of people who are crooked and stubborn. Shine out among them like beacon lights, holding out to them the Word of Life.

Let everyone see that you are unselfish and considerate in all you do.

Philippians 1:27. Philippians 2:12-16. Philippians 4:5.

PHILIPPIANS

I want you always to see clearly the difference between right and wrong.

And to be inwardly clean, no one being able to criticize you from now until our Lord returns.

Don't be selfish; don't live to make a good impression on others. Be humble, thinking of others as better than yourself. Don't just think about your own affairs, but be interested in others too, and in what they are doing.

Christ, who suffered for you, is your example. Follow in his steps: He never sinned, never told a lie, never answered back when insulted. When he suffered he did not threaten to get even; he left his case in the hands of God who always judges fairly.

Philippians 1:10. Philippians 2:3, 4. 1 Peter 2:21-23.

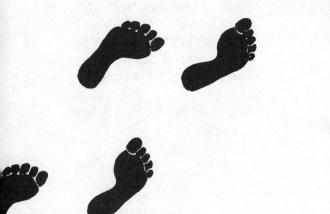

Your attitude should be the kind that was shown us by Jesus Christ.

Treat others as you want them to treat you. Do you think you deserve credit for merely loving those who love you? Even the godless do that! And if you do good only to those who do you good—is that so wonderful? Even sinners do that much!

And if you lend money only to those who can repay you, what good is that? Even the most wicked will lend to their own kind for full return! Love your enemies! Do good to them! Lend to them! And don't be concerned about the fact that they won't repay. Then your reward from heaven will be very great, and you will truly be acting as sons of God.

Philippians 1:11. Philippians 2:5. Luke 6:31-35.

Always be doing those good, kind things which show that you are a child of God.

PHILIPPIANS

Overflow more and more with love for others.

Don't let anyone
think little of you because
you are young. Be their ideal;
let them follow the way
you teach and live.
Be a pattern for them
in your love, your faith,
and your clean thoughts.

Don't just pretend that you love others: really love
them. Hate what is wrong. Stand on the side of the good.
Love each other with brotherly affection and take
delight in honoring each other.

How wonderful it is, how pleasant when brothers live
in harmony!

Philippians 1:9. 1 Timothy 4:12. Romans 12:9, 10. Psalm 133:1.

Instead, pray about everything. Tell God your needs and don't forget to thank him for his answers. If you do this you will experience God's peace, which is far more wonderful than the human mind can understand. His peace will keep your thoughts and your hearts quiet and at rest as you trust in Christ Jesus.

Whatever happens, dear friends, be glad in the Lord.

The Lord lifts the fallen and those bent beneath their loads. The eyes of all mankind look up to you for help; you give them their food as they need it. You constantly satisfy the hunger and thirst of every living thing.

Those who trust in the Lord are steady as Mount Zion, unmoved by any circumstance.

Don't worry about anything.

Philippians 4:6, 7. Philippians 3:1. Psalm 145:14-16. Psalm 125:1.

PHILIPPIANS

**He will supply
all your needs
from his riches in glory,
because of what Christ
Jesus has done for us.**

Because the Lord is my Shepherd, I
have everything I need!
For Jehovah God is our Light and
our Protector. He gives us grace and
glory. No good thing will he withhold
from those who walk along his paths.
The living God . . . richly gives us all
we need for our enjoyment.
God is able to make it up to you by
giving you everything you need and
more, so that there will not
only be enough for your own
needs, but plenty left over
to give joyfully to others.
Since he did not spare even
his own Son for us but gave him
up for us all, won't he also surely
give us everything
else?

Philippians 4:19. Psalm 23:1.
Psalm 84:11.
1 Timothy 6:17. 2 Corinthians 9:8.
Romans 8:32.

Christ has brought you into the very presence of God.

The only condition is that you fully believe the Truth, standing in it steadfast and firm, strong in the Lord, convinced of the Good News that Jesus died for you, and never shifting from trusting him to save you.

Just as you trusted Christ to save you, trust him, too, for each day's problems; live in vital union with him. Let your roots grow down into him and draw up nourishment from him.

Remember what Christ taught and let his words enrich your lives and make you wise. Teach them to each other and sing them out in psalms and hymns and spiritual songs, singing to the Lord with thankful hearts.

Colossians 1:22, 23. Colossians 2:6, 7. Colossians 3:16.

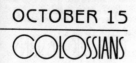
COLOSSIANS

Christ
in your hearts
is your only hope
of glory.

Christ is the exact likeness of the unseen God.
He existed before God made anything at all,
and, in fact, Christ himself is the Creator who
made everything in heaven and earth, the
things we can see and the things we can't.
He was before all else began and it is his
power that holds everything together.
He is the Head of the body made up of his
people—that is, his church—which he began.
Christ's death on the cross has made peace
with God for all by his blood.

This includes you.

Colossians 1:27, 15-18, 20, 21.

COLOSSIANS

In him (Christ) lie hidden all the mighty, untapped treasures of wisdom and knowledge.

This is what I have asked of God for you: that you will be encouraged and knit together by strong ties of love, and that you will have the rich experience of knowing Christ with real certainty and clear understanding.

. . . Asking God to help you understand what he wants you to do, asking him to make you wise about spiritual things; and asking that the way you live will always please the Lord and honor him, so that you will always be doing good, kind things for others, while all the time you are learning to know God better and better.

Colossians 2:3, 2. Colossians 1:9, 10.

You have everything when you have Christ.

Don't let others spoil your faith and joy with their philosophies, their wrong and shallow answers built on men's thoughts and ideas, instead of on what Christ has said.

Don't let anyone declare you lost when you refuse to worship angels as they say you must. They have seen a vision, they say, and know you should. These proud men (though they claim to be so humble) have a very clear imagination. But they are not connected to Christ.

Stay away from those who cause divisions and are upsetting people's faith, teaching things about Christ that are contrary to what you have been taught.

We grow only as we get our nourishment and strength from God.

Colossians 2:10, 8, 18, 19. Romans 16:17.
Colossians 2:19.

COLOSSIANS

**Let heaven
fill your thoughts.**

You should have as little desire for this world as a dead person does. Your real life is in heaven with Christ and God. And when Christ who is our real life comes back again, you will shine with him and share in all his glories.

Set your sights on the rich treasures and joys of heaven where he sits beside God in the place of honor and power.

Don't be weary in prayer; keep at it; watch for God's answers and remember to be thankful when they come.

And whatever you do or say, let it be as a representative of the Lord Jesus.

Colossians 3:2-4, 1. Colossians 4:2. Colossians 3:17.

Be sure that you do all the Lord has told you to.

Don't tell lies to each other. It was your old life with all its wickedness that did that sort of thing. Now it is dead and gone. You are living a brand new kind of life that is continually learning more and more of what is right, and trying constantly to be more and more like Christ who created this new life within you.

Don't worry about making a good impression ... but be ready to suffer quietly and patiently. Be gentle and ready to forgive; never hold grudges. Remember, the Lord forgave you, so you must forgive others.

Colossians 4:17. Colossians 3:9, 10, 12, 13.

1&2 THESSALONIANS

God will make you the kind of children he wants to have— will make you as good as you wish you could be!

Your daily lives should not embarrass God, but bring joy to him who invited you into his kingdom to share his glory.

You already know how to please God in your daily living, for you know the commands . . . live more and more closely to that ideal.

Every spiritual gift and power for doing his will are yours during this time of waiting for the return of our Lord Jesus Christ. And he guarantees right up to the end that you will be counted free from all sin and guilt on that day when he returns.

2 Thessalonians 1:11. 1 Thessalonians 2:12. 1 Thessalonians 4:1, 2. 1 Corinthians 1:7,8.

Troubles are a part of God's plan for us Christians.

We are happy . . . about your patience and complete faith in God, in spite of all the crushing troubles and hardships you are going through. This is only one example of the fair, just ways God does things, for he is using your sufferings to make you ready for his kingdom.

Of course you get no credit for being patient if you are beaten for doing wrong, but if you do right and suffer for it, and are patient beneath the blows, God is well pleased.

Keep on doing what is right and trust yourself to the God who made you, for he will never fail you.

1 Thessalonians 3:3. 2 Thessalonians 1:4, 5. 1 Peter 2:20. 1 Peter 4:19.

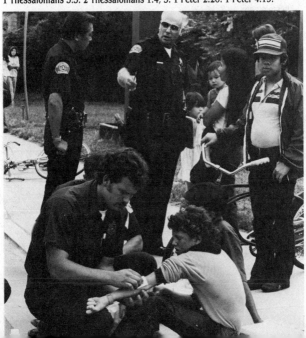

1&2 THESSALONIANS

I want you to know what happens to a Christian when he dies so that when it happens, you will not be full of sorrow, as those are who have no hope. For since we believe that Jesus died and then came back to life again, we can also believe that when Jesus returns, God will bring back with him all the Christians who have died.

We who are still living when the Lord returns will not rise to meet him ahead of those who are in their graves. The believers who are dead will be the first to rise to meet the Lord. Then we who are still alive and remain on the earth will be caught up with them in the clouds to meet the Lord in the air and remain with him forever.

1 Thessalonians 4:18, 13-17.

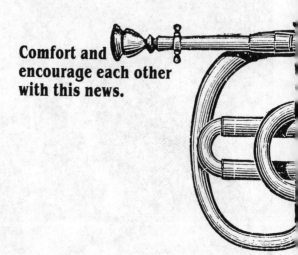

Comfort and encourage each other with this news.

When is all this going to happen?

No one knows. That day of the Lord will come unexpectedly like a thief in the night ... with a mighty shout and with the soul-stirring cry of the archangel and the great trumpet-call of God.

There will be great joy for those who are ready and waiting for his return. He himself will seat them and put on a waiter's uniform and serve them as they sit and eat! He may come at nine o'clock at night—or even at midnight. But whenever he comes there will be joy for his servants who are ready! Everyone would be ready for him if they knew the exact hour of his return—just as they would be ready for a thief if they knew when he was coming. So be ready all the time.

1 Thessalonians 5:1, 2. Luke 12:37-40.
1 Thessalonians 4:16.

1&2 THESSALONIANS

This should be your ambition: to live a quiet life, minding your own business and doing your own work. Warn those who are lazy; comfort those who are frightened; take tender care of those who are weak; and be patient with everyone. See that no one pays back evil for evil, but always try to do good to each other and to everyone else. Always be joyful. Always keep on praying. No matter what happens, always be thankful, for this is God's will for you who belong to Christ Jesus.

This will result in your hearts being made strong, sinless and holy by God our Father, so that you may stand before him guiltless on that day when our Lord Jesus Christ returns with all those who belong to him.

1 Thessalonians 3:10.
1 Thessalonians 4:11.
1 Thessalonians 5:14-18.
1 Thessalonians 3:13.

Fill up any little cracks there may yet be in your faith.

**Stand firm
and keep a strong grip
on the truth.**

1 & 2 THESSALONIANS

Honor the officers of your church who work hard among you and warn you against all that is wrong. Think highly of them and give them your wholehearted love because they are straining to help you. Obey your spiritual leaders and be willing to do what they say. Give them reason to report joyfully about you to the Lord and not with sorrow, for then you will suffer for it too.

Don't let the excitement of being young cause you to forget about your Creator!

2 Thessalonians 2:15. 1 Thessalonians 5:12, 13. Hebrews 13:17.
Ecclesiastes 12:1.

1 TIMOTHY

Cling tightly to your faith in Christ.

Always keep your conscience clear, doing what you know is right. For some people have disobeyed their consciences and have deliberately done what they knew was wrong.

Pray much for others. Plead for God's mercy upon them. Give thanks for all he is going to do for them.

Pray in this way for kings and all others who are in authority over us, or are in places of high responsibility so that we can live in peace and quietness, spending our time in godly living and thinking much about the Lord.

1 Timothy 1:19. 1 Timothy 2:1, 2.

God is on one side and all the people on the other side, and Christ Jesus, himself man, is between them to bring them together.

It was necessary for Jesus to be like us ... so that he could be our merciful and faithful High Priest before God, a Priest who would be both merciful to us and faithful to God in dealing with the sins of the people.

Jesus the Son of God is our great High Priest who has gone to heaven itself to help us; therefore let us never stop trusting him. This High Priest of ours understands our weaknesses, since he had the same temptations we do.

1 Timothy 2:5. Hebrews 2:17. Hebrews 4:14, 15.

1 TIMOTHY

Spend your time and energy in the exercise of keeping spiritually fit.

Bodily exercise is all right, but spiritual exercise is much more important and is a tonic for all you do. So exercise yourself spiritually and practice being a better Christian, because that will help you not only now in this life, but in the next life too.

In a race, everyone runs but only one person gets first prize. So run your race to win. To win the contest you must deny yourselves many things that would keep you from doing your best. An athlete goes to all this trouble just to win a blue ribbon or a silver cup, but we do it for a heavenly reward that never disappears.

1 Timothy 4:7, 8. 1 Corinthians 9:24, 25.

1 TIMOTHY

Hard work means prosperity; only a fool idles away his time. Work hard and become a leader; be lazy and never succeed. A lazy man won't even dress the game he gets while hunting, but the diligent man makes good use of everything he finds.

Be sure to use the abilities God has given you. Put these abilities to work; throw yourself into your tasks so that everyone may notice your improvement and progress. Keep a close watch on all you do and think. Stay true to what is right and God will bless you and use you to help others.

Proverbs 22:29. Proverbs 12:11, 24, 27. 1 Timothy 4:14-16.

Do you know a hard-working man? He shall be successful and stand before kings!

1 TIMOTHY

You must respect your mothers and fathers.

You shall give due honor and respect to the elderly, in the fear of God. I am Jehovah. Never speak sharply to an older man, but plead with him respectfully just as though he were your own father. Talk to the younger men as you would to much loved brothers.

Treat the older women as mothers, and the girls as your sisters, thinking only pure thoughts about them.

Don't let anyone think little of you because you are young. Be their ideal; let them follow the way you teach and live; be a pattern for them in your love, your faith, and your clean thoughts.

Leviticus 19:2, 32.
1 Timothy 5:1, 2.
1 Timothy 4:12.

1 TIMOTHY

The Holy Spirit tells us clearly that in the last times some in the church will turn away from Christ and become eager followers of teachers with devil-inspired ideas. These teachers will tell lies with straight faces and

Beware of false teachers who come disguised as harmless sheep.

do it so often that their consciences won't even bother them. They will say it is wrong to be married and wrong to eat meat, even though God gave these things to well-taught Christians to enjoy and be thankful for.

For everything God made is good, and we may eat it gladly if we are thankful for it, and if we ask God to bless it, for it is made good by the Word of God and prayer.

Matthew 7:15. 1 Timothy 4:1-5.

Do you want to be truly rich? You already are if you are happy and good. After all, we didn't bring any money with us when we came into the world, and we can't carry away a single penny when we die.

So we should be well satisfied without money if we have enough food and clothing. But people who long to be rich soon begin to do all kinds of wrong things to get money, things that hurt them and make them evil-minded and finally send them to hell itself.

For the love of money is the first step toward all kinds of sin.

Ecclesiastes 5:10. 1 Timothy 6:6-10.

He who loves money shall never have enough.

1 TIMOTHY

**Trust in your money
and down you go!
Trust in God
and flourish as a tree!**

Tell those who are rich not to be
proud and not to trust in their
money, which will soon be gone,
but their pride and trust should
be in the living God who always
richly gives us all we need for
our enjoyment.
Tell them to use their money
to do good. They should be rich
in good works and should give
happily to those in need, always
being ready to share with others
whatever God has given them.
By doing this they will be storing
up real treasure for themselves
in heaven—it is the only safe
investment for eternity! And
they will be living a fruitful
Christian life down here as well.

Proverbs 11:28. 1 Timothy 6:17-19.

1 TIMOTHY

Fight on for God.

Hold tightly to the eternal life which God has given you. Work . . . at what is right and good, learning to trust him and love others, and to be patient and gentle.

Fulfill all he has told you to do, so that no one can find fault with you from now until our Lord Jesus Christ returns. For in due season Christ will be revealed from heaven by the blessed and only Almighty God, the King of kings and Lord of lords, who alone can never die, who lives in light so terrible no human being can approach him. No mere man has ever seen him, nor ever will.

Unto him be honor and everlasting power and dominion forever and ever. Amen.

1 Timothy 6:12, 11, 14-16.

2 TIMOTHY

Cheer up!
Take courage if you
are depending on the Lord.

The Holy Spirit, God's gift, does not
want you to be afraid of people, but to
be wise and strong, and to love them
and enjoy being with them. If you will
stir up this inner power, you will never
be afraid to tell others about our Lord.

Do not let yourself become tied up
in worldly affairs, for then you cannot
satisfy the one who enlisted you in his
army. Follow the Lord's rule for doing
his work, just as an athlete either
follows the rules or is disqualified and
wins no prize. Work hard, like a farmer
who gets paid well if he raises a large
crop.

The righteous shall move onward
and forward; those with pure hearts
shall become stronger and stronger.

Psalm 31:24. 2 Timothy 1:7, 8. 2 Timothy 2:4-6.
Job 17:9.

2 TIMOTHY

A person who calls himself a Christian should not be doing things that are wrong.

In a wealthy home there are dishes made of gold and silver as well as some made from wood and clay. The expensive dishes are used for guests, and the cheap ones are used in the kitchen or to put garbage in. If you stay away from sin you will be like one of these dishes made of purest gold—the very best in the house—so that Christ himself can use you for his highest purposes.

Don't get involved in foolish arguments which only upset people and make them angry. God's people must not be quarrelsome. They must be gentle, patient teachers of those who are wrong.

2 Timothy 2:19-21, 23, 24.

Keep on believing the things you have been taught.

You know they are true for you know that you can trust those of us who have taught you.

You know how, when you were a small child, you were taught the holy Scriptures; and it is these that make you wise to accept God's salvation by trusting in Christ Jesus.

The whole Bible was given to us by inspiration from God and is useful to teach us what is true and to make us realize what is wrong in our lives. It straightens us out and helps us do what is right. It is God's way of making us well prepared at every point, fully equipped to do good to everyone.

2 Timothy 3:14-17.

2 TIMOTHY

The crown of life— an unending, glorious future.

I have fought long and hard for my Lord, and through it all I have kept true to him. And now the time has come for me to stop fighting and rest. In heaven a crown is waiting for me which the Lord, the righteous Judge, will give me on that great day of his return. And not just to me, but to all those whose lives show that they are eagerly looking forward to his coming back again.

Happy is the man who doesn't give in and do wrong when he is tempted, for afterwards he will get as his reward the crown of life that God has promised those who love him.

Revelation 2:10. 2 Timothy 4:7, 8. James 1:12.

TITUS

Be an example . . . of good deeds of every kind.

Let everything you do reflect your love of the truth and the fact that you are in dead earnest about it. Your conversation should be so sensible and logical that anyone who wants to argue will be ashamed of himself because there won't be anything to criticize in anything you say!

Try to show as much compassion as your Father does. Never criticize or condemn— or it will all come back on you. Go easy on others; then they will do the same for you.

Titus 2:7, 8. Luke 6:36.

TITUS

A person who is pure of heart sees goodness and purity in everything.

But a person whose own heart is evil and untrusting finds evil in everything, for his dirty mind and rebellious heart color all he sees and hears.

Who may climb the mountain of the Lord and enter where he lives? Who may stand before the Lord? Only those with pure hands and hearts, who do not practice dishonesty and lying.

Fix your thoughts on what is true and good and right. Think about things that are pure and lovely, and dwell on the fine, good things in others. Think about all you can praise God for and be glad about.

Titus 1:15. Psalm 24:3, 4. Philippians 4:8.

TITUS

Obey the government and its officers.

Obey the government, for God is the one who has put it there. There is no government anywhere that God has not placed in power. So those who refuse to obey the laws of the land are refusing to obey God, and punishment will follow.

For the policeman does not frighten people who are doing right; but those doing evil will always fear him.

The policeman is sent by God to help you. But if you are doing something wrong, of course you should be afraid, for he will have you punished. He is sent by God for that very purpose.

Obey the laws, then, for two reasons: first, to keep from being punished, and second, just because you know you should.

Titus 3:1. Romans 13:1-5.

PHILEMON

Show kindness to my child Onesimus.

Onesimus (whose name means "Useful") hasn't been of much use to you in the past. He ran away from you for a little while. Rebuke your brother if he sins, and forgive him if he is sorry. Even if he wrongs you seven times a day and each time turns again and asks forgiveness, forgive him.

Never pay back evil for evil. Do things in such a way that everyone can see you are honest clear through.

Be gentle and ready to forgive; never hold grudges. Remember, the Lord forgave you, so you must forgive others.

Happy are the kind and merciful, for they shall be shown mercy.

Philemon 10, 11, 15. Luke 17:3, 4.
Romans 12:17. Colossians 3:13.
Matthew 5:7.

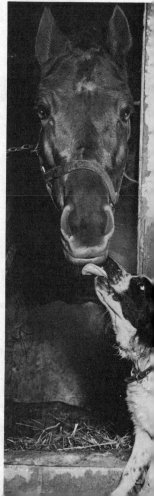

HEBREWS

All that God's Son is and does marks him as God.

He regulates the universe by the mighty power of his command.

He is the one who died to cleanse us and clear our record of all sin.

He became far greater than the angels. God said, "Let all the angels of God worship him."

God speaks of his angels as messengers swift as the wind and as servants made of flaming fire; but of his Son he says, "Your kingdom, O God, will last forever and ever; its commands are always just and right. You love right and hate wrong; so God, even your God, has poured out more gladness upon you than on anyone else."

God also called him "Lord" when he said, "Lord, in the beginning you made the earth, and the heavens are the work of your hands. You, yourself will never change, and your years will never end."

Hebrews 1:3, 4, 6-10, 12.

HEBREWS

**Christ said . . .
"Here I am.
I have come
to give my life."**

Christ gave himself to God for
our sins as one sacrifice for all
time, and then sat down in the
place of highest honor at God's
right hand waiting for his
enemies to be laid under his
feet. For by that one offering he
made forever perfect in the sight
of God all those whom he is
making holy.

His sacrifice frees us from the
worry of having to obey the old
rules, and makes us want to
serve the living God.

Christ came . . . so that all
who are invited may come and
have forever all the wonders God
has promised them.

Hebrews 10:8, 9, 12-14. Hebrews 9:14, 15.

HEBREWS

The life of the flesh is in the blood.

In fact we can say that under the old agreement almost everything was cleansed by sprinkling it with blood, and without the shedding of blood there is no forgiveness of sins.

That is why Jesus suffered and died outside the city, where his blood washed our sins away.

His sacrifice frees us from the worry of having to obey the old rules, and makes us want to serve the living God. For by the help of the eternal Holy Spirit, Christ willingly gave himself to God to die for our sins—he being perfect, without a single sin or fault.

So you see, our love for him comes as a result of his loving us first. And as we live with Christ, our love grows more perfect and complete.

Leviticus 17:11. Hebrews 9:22. Hebrews 13:12. Hebrews 9:14. 1 John 4:19, 17.

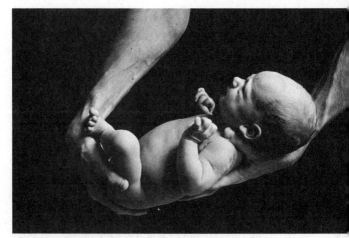

He did not come as an angel but as a human being.

It was necessary for Jesus to be like us, his brothers, so that he could be our merciful and faithful High Priest before God, a Priest who would be both merciful to us and faithful to God in dealing with the sins of the people. For since he himself has now been through suffering and temptation, he knows what it is like when we suffer and are tempted, and he is wonderfully able to help us.

And it was right and proper that God, who made everything for his own glory, should allow Jesus to suffer, for in doing this he was bringing vast multitudes of God's people to heaven; for his suffering made Jesus a perfect Leader, one fit to bring them into their salvation.

Hebrews 2:16-18, 10.

HEBREWS

Jesus lives forever and continues to be a Priest so that no one else is needed.

He is able to save completely all who come to God through him. Since he will live forever, he will always be there to remind God that he has paid for their sins with his blood.

He is, therefore, exactly the kind of High Priest we need; for he is holy and blameless, unstained by sin, undefiled by sinners, and to him has been given the place of honor in heaven.

To him belongs the royal title. He will rule both as King and as Priest, with perfect harmony between the two!

Hebrews 7:24-26. Zechariah 6:13.

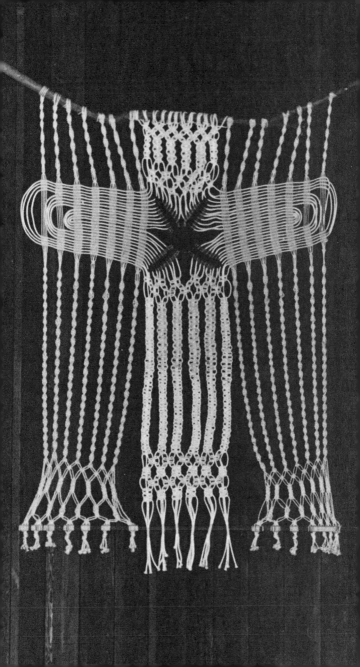

HEBREWS

Run with patience the particular race that God has set before us.

Let us strip off anything that slows us down or holds us back, and especially those sins that wrap themselves so tightly around our feet and trip us up.

Let God train you, for he is doing what any loving father does for his children. Whoever heard of a son who was never corrected? If God doesn't punish you when you need it . . . then it means that you aren't really God's son at all—that you don't really belong in his family. Since we respect our fathers here on earth, though they punish us, should we not all the more cheerfully submit to God's training so that we can begin really to live?

Keep your eyes on Jesus, our leader and instructor.

Hebrews 12:1, 7-9, 2.

You have given us your laws to obey— oh, how I want to follow them consistently.

Whatever God says to us is full of living power. It is sharper than the sharpest dagger, cutting swift and deep into our innermost thoughts and desires with all their parts, exposing us for what we really are.

He knows about everyone, everywhere. Everything about us is bare and wide open to the all-seeing eyes of our living God. Nothing can be hidden from him to whom we must explain all that we have done.

After you have corrected me I will thank you by living as I should! I will obey!

Psalm 119:4. Hebrews 4:12, 13.
Psalm 119:7, 8.

HEBREWS

**God's correction
is always right
and for our best good,
that we may share
his holiness.**

Being punished isn't enjoyable while it is happening—it hurts! But afterwards we can see the result, a quiet growth in grace and character.

So take a new grip with your tired hands, stand firm on your shaky legs, and mark out a straight, smooth path for your feet so that those who follow you, though weak and lame, will not fall and hurt themselves, but become strong.

Try to stay out of all quarrels and seek to live a clean and holy life, for one who is not holy will not see the Lord. Look after each other so that not one of you will fail to find God's best blessings.

Hebrews 12:10-15.

Continue to love each other with true brotherly love.

Don't forget to be kind to strangers, for some who have done this have entertained angels without realizing it! Don't forget about those in jail. Suffer with them as though you were there yourself. Share the sorrow of those being mistreated.

Don't forget to do good and to share what you have with those in need, for such sacrifices are very pleasing to him (Jesus).

And now may the God of peace, who brought again from the dead our Lord Jesus, equip you with all you need for doing his will.

Hebrews 13:1-3, 16, 20.

JAMES

God is good and he loves goodness.

Whatever is good and perfect comes to us from God, the Creator of all light, and he shines forever without change or shadow.

And it was a happy day for him when he gave us our new lives, through the truth of his Word, and we became, as it were, the first children in his new family.

What a glorious Lord! He who daily bears our burdens also gives us our salvation.

He is good to everyone and his compassion is intertwined with everything he does.

When trouble comes, he is the place to go! And he knows everyone who trusts in him!

For God is love.

Psalm 11:7. James 1:17, 18. Psalm 68:19.
Psalm 145:9. Nahum 1:7. 1 John 4:8.

JAMES

Is your life full of difficulties and temptations?

Then be happy, for when the way is rough, your patience has a chance to grow. So let it grow, and don't try to squirm out of your problems. For when your patience is finally in full bloom, then you will be ready for anything, strong in character, full and complete.

Remember this—the wrong desires that come into your life aren't anything new and different. Many others have faced exactly the same problems before you. And no temptation is irresistible. You can trust God to keep the temptation from becoming so strong that you can't stand up against it.

James 1:2-4, 1 Corinthians 10:13.

JAMES

**Don't act thoughtlessly,
but try to find out
and do whatever
the Lord wants you to.**

If you want to know what God wants you to do, ask him, and he will gladly tell you, for he is always ready to give a bountiful supply of wisdom to all who ask him; he will not resent it.

But when you ask him, be sure that you really expect him to tell you, for a doubtful mind will be as unsettled as a wave of the sea that is driven and tossed by the wind; and every decision you then make will be uncertain, as you turn first this way, and then that.

If you don't ask with faith, don't expect the Lord to give you any solid answer.

Ephesians 5:17. James 1:5-8.

JAMES

It is best to listen much, speak little, and not become angry.

Anger doesn't make us good, as God demands that we must be.

So get rid of all that is wrong in your life, both inside and outside, and humbly be glad for the wonderful message we have received, for it is able to save our souls as it takes hold of our hearts.

And remember, it is a message to obey, not just to listen to. So don't fool yourselves. For if a person just listens and doesn't obey, he is like a man looking at his face in a mirror; as soon as he walks away, he can't see himself anymore or remember what he looks like.

But if anyone keeps looking steadily into God's law for free men, he will not only remember it but he will do what it says, and God will greatly bless him in everything he does.

James 1:19-25.

JAMES

Watch your tongue!
Keep your lips from lying.

If anyone can control his tongue, it proves that he has perfect control over himself in every other way.

We can make a large horse turn around and go wherever we want by means of a small bit in his mouth. Men have trained, or can train, every kind of animal or bird that lives and every kind of reptile and fish, but no human being can tame the tongue. What enormous damage it can do! A great forest can be set on fire by one tiny spark. And the tongue . . . can turn our whole lives into a blazing flame of destruction and disaster.

A soft answer turns away wrath, but harsh words cause quarrels. Gentle words cause life and health; griping brings discouragement.

Psalm 34:13. James 3:2,3,7,8,5,6. Proverbs 15:1,4.

JAMES

Are there still some among you who hold that "only believing" is enough?

Good works are important too, for without good works you can't prove whether you have faith or not.

It isn't enough just to have faith. You must also do good to prove that you have it. Faith that doesn't show itself by good works is no faith at all—it is dead and useless.

What's the use of saying that you have faith and are Christians if you aren't proving it by helping others? Will *that* kind of faith save anyone? If you have a friend who is in need of food and clothing, and you say to him, "Well, good-bye and God bless you; stay warm and eat hearty," and then don't give him clothes or food, what good does that do?

Faith that does not result in good deeds is not real faith.

James 2:19,18,17,14-16,20.

Van Gogh, *The Good Samaritan*, Rijksmuseum Kroller-Muller, Otterlo, Netherlands

JAMES

If you are wise, live a life of steady goodness, so that only good deeds will pour forth.

And if you don't brag about them, then you will be truly wise!

And by all means don't brag about being wise and good if you are bitter and jealous and selfish; that is the worst sort of lie. For jealousy and selfishness are not God's kind of wisdom. Such things are earthly, unspiritual, inspired by the devil. For wherever there is jealousy or selfish ambition, there will be disorder and every other kind of evil.

But the wisdom that comes from heaven is first of all pure and full of quiet gentleness. Then it is peace-loving and courteous. It allows discussion and is willing to yield to others; it is full of mercy and good deeds. It is wholehearted and straightforward and sincere. And those who are peacemakers will plant seeds of peace and reap a harvest of goodness.

James 3:13-18.

JAMES

**It is better
to have little
and be godly.**

A Christian who doesn't amount to much
in this world should be glad, for he is great
in the Lord's sight.
A rich man should be glad that his riches mean
nothing to the Lord, for he will soon be gone, like a
flower that has lost its beauty and fades away,
withered—killed by the scorching summer sun. So it is
with rich men. They will soon die and leave behind all
their busy activities.
Some rich people are poor, and some poor people have
great wealth! God has chosen poor people to be rich in
faith, and the Kingdom of Heaven is theirs, for that is
the gift God has promised to all those who love him.
Beware! Don't always be wishing
for what you don't have.

Psalm 37:16. James 1:9-11. Proverbs 13:7. James 2:5.
Luke 12:15.

1 PETER

Obey God because you are his children.

Don't slip back into your old ways—doing evil because you knew no better. But be holy now in everything you do, just as the Lord is holy, who invited you to be his child. He himself has said, "You must be holy, for I am holy."

And remember that your heavenly Father to whom you pray has no favorites when he judges. He will judge you with perfect justice for everything you do; so act in reverent fear of him from now on until you get to heaven.

1 Peter 1:14-17.

1 PETER

**I am sending Christ
to be the carefully chosen,
precious Cornerstone of my church,
and I will never disappoint
those who trust in him.**

You are priests of the King, you are holy and pure, you are God's very own—all this so that you may show to others how God called you out of the darkness into his wonderful light. Once you were less than nothing; now you are God's own. Once you knew very little of God's kindness; now your very lives have been changed by it.

For you have a new life. It was not passed on to you from your parents, for the life they gave you will fade away. This new one will last forever, for it comes from Christ, God's ever-living Message to men.

1 Peter 2:6,9,10. 1 Peter 1:23.

1 PETER

**You are only visitors here . . .
keep away from the evil pleasures
of this world.**

Be careful how you behave among your
unsaved neighbors; for then, even if they are
suspicious of you and talk against you, they
will end up praising God for your good works
when Christ returns.

It is God's will that your good lives should
silence those who foolishly condemn the Gospel
without knowing what it can do for them,
having never experienced its power. You are
free from the law, but that doesn't mean you
are free to do wrong. Live as those who are free
to do only God's will at all times.

Show respect for everyone. Love Christians
everywhere. Fear God and honor the
government.

1 Peter 2:11, 12, 15-17.

Love each other warmly, with all your hearts.

You should be like one big happy family, full of sympathy toward each other, loving one another with tender hearts and humble minds.

Don't repay evil for evil. Don't snap back at those who say unkind things about you. Instead, pray for God's help for them, for we are to be kind to others, and God will bless us for it.

If you want a happy, good life, keep control of your tongue, and guard your lips from telling lies. Turn away from evil and do good. Try to live in peace even if you must run after it to catch and hold it!

1 Peter 1:22. 1 Peter 3:8-11.

Usually no one will hurt you for wanting to do good.

But even if they should, you are to be envied, for God will reward you for it. Quietly trust yourself to Christ your Lord and if anybody asks why you believe as you do, be ready to tell him, and do it in a gentle and respectful way. Do what is right; then if men speak against you, calling you evil names, they will become ashamed of themselves for falsely accusing you when you have only done what is good. Remember, if God wants you to suffer, it is better to suffer for doing good than for doing wrong!

1 Peter 3:13-17.

Be happy if you are cursed and insulted for being a Christian.

Don't let me hear of your suffering for murdering or stealing or making trouble or being a busybody and prying into other people's affairs.

But it is no shame to suffer for being a Christian. Praise God for the privilege of being in Christ's family and being called by his wonderful name!

Since Christ suffered and underwent pain, you must have the same attitude he did; you must be ready to suffer, too. After you have suffered a little while, our God, who is full of kindness through Christ, will give you his eternal glory.

1 Peter 4:14-16, 1. 1 Peter 5:10.

2 PETER

**Work hard
to prove that
you really are
among those God
has called and chosen.**

Then you will never stumble or
fall away. And God will open
wide the gates of heaven for you
to enter into the eternal
kingdom of our Lord and Savior
Jesus Christ.
The day of the Lord is surely
coming, as unexpectedly as a
thief, and then the heavens will
pass away with a terrible noise
and the heavenly bodies will
disappear in fire, and the earth
and everything on it will be
burned up.
And so since everything around
us is going to melt away, what
holy, godly lives we should be
living!

2 Peter 1:10, 11. 2 Peter 3:10, 11.

2 PETER

Rich and wonderful blessings he promised.

But to obtain these gifts, you need more than faith; you must also work hard to be good, and even that is not enough. For then you must learn to know God better and discover what he wants you to do.

Next, learn to put aside your own desires so that you will become patient and godly, gladly letting God have his way with you.

This will make possible the next step, which is for you to enjoy other people and to like them, and finally you will grow to love them deeply. The more you go on in this way, the more you will grow spiritually and become fruitful and useful to our Lord Jesus Christ.

2 Peter 1:4-8.

Looking forward to God's promise of new heavens and a new earth.

First, I want to remind you that in the last days there will come scoffers who will do every wrong they can think of, and laugh at the truth.

This will be their line of argument: "So Jesus promised to come back, did he? Then where is he? He'll never come! Why, as far back as anyone can remember everything has remained exactly as it was since the first day of creation."

But don't forget ... that a day or a thousand years from now is like tomorrow to the Lord. He isn't really being slow about his promised return, even though it sometimes seems that way. But he is waiting, for the good reason that he is not willing that any should perish, and he is giving more time for sinners to repent.

Be at peace with everyone so that he will be pleased with you when he returns.

2 Peter 3:13, 3, 4, 8, 9, 14.

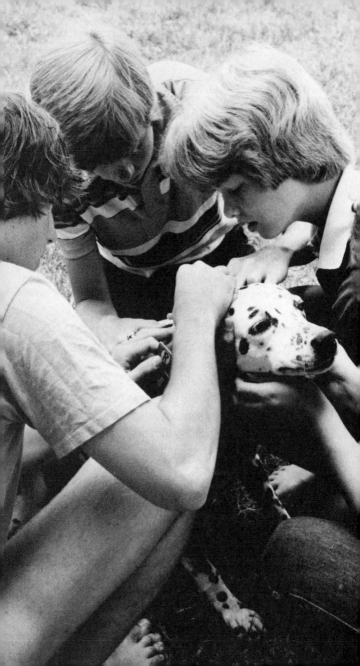

Practice loving each other.

Love comes from God and those who are loving and kind show that they are the children of God, and that they are getting to know him better.

If someone who is supposed to be a Christian has money enough to live well, and sees a brother in need, and won't help him—how can God's love be within him? Let us stop just saying we love people; let us really love them, and show it by our actions. Then we will know for sure, by our actions, that we are on God's side, and our consciences will be clear, even when we stand before the Lord.

If, as my representatives, you give even a cup of cold water to a little child, you will surely be rewarded.

1 John 4:7. 1 John 3:17-19. Matthew 10:42.

1 JOHN

God is Light and in him is no darkness at all.

For Jehovah God is our Light and Protector.

In one of his talks, Jesus said to the people, "I am the Light of the world. So if you follow me, you won't be stumbling through the darkness, for living light will flood your path."

For though once your heart was full of darkness, now it is full of light from the Lord, and your behavior should show it!

You are to live clean, innocent lives as children of God in a dark world full of people who are crooked and stubborn. Shine out among them like beacon lights. So that no one can speak a word of blame against you.

1 John 1:5. Psalm 84:11. John 8:12.
Ephesians 5:8. Philippians 2:15.

1 JOHN

The blood of Jesus his Son cleanses us from every sin.

If we confess our sins to him, he can be depended on to forgive us and to cleanse us from every wrong.

It will be as though I had sprinkled clean water on you, for you will be clean. And I will give you a new heart—I will give you new and right desires—and put a new spirit within you. I

 will take out your stony hearts of sin and give you new hearts of love. And I will put my Spirit within you so that you will obey my laws and do whatever I command.

Be full of love for others, following the example of Christ who loved you and gave himself to God as a sacrifice to take away your sins.

1 John 1:7, 9. Ezekiel 36:25-27. Ephesians 5:2.

1 JOHN

**Someone may say,
"I am a Christian.
I am on my way to heaven.
I belong to Christ."**

And how can we be sure that we
belong to him? By looking within
ourselves: are we really trying to do
what he wants us to?

Those who do what Christ tells them
to will learn to love God more and
more. That is the way to know whether
or not you are a Christian.

I am not writing out a new rule for
you to obey, for it is an old one you
have always had, right from the start.
You have heard it all before. Yet it is
always new, and works for you just as
it did for Christ; and as we obey this
commandment, *to love one another*,
the darkness in our lives disappears
and the new light of life in Christ
shines in.

1 John 2:4, 3, 5-8.

Anyone who says he is a Christian should live as Christ did.

Don't hide your light! Let it shine for all; let your good deeds glow for all to see, so that they will praise your heavenly Father.

Your godly lives will speak to them better than words. Don't be concerned about the outward beauty that depends on jewelry, or beautiful clothes, or hair arrangement. Be beautiful inside, in your hearts, with the lasting charm of a gentle and quiet spirit which is so precious to God.

You should be like one big happy family, full of sympathy toward each other, loving one another with tender hearts and humble minds.

1 John 2:6. Matthew 5:15, 16. 1 Peter 3:2-4, 8.

1 JOHN

We can tell who is a child of God and who belongs to Satan.

Whoever is living a life of sin and doesn't love his brother shows that he is not in God's family; for the message to us from the beginning has been that we should love one another.

We are not to be like Cain, who belonged to Satan and killed his brother. Why did he kill him? Because Cain had been doing wrong and he knew very well that his brother's life was better than his.

If we love other Christians it proves that we have been delivered from hell and given eternal life. But a person who doesn't have love for others is headed for eternal death. Anyone who hates his Christian brother is really a murderer at heart; and you know that no one wanting to murder has eternal life within.

We know what real love is from Christ's example in dying for us.

1 John 3:10-12, 14-16.

1 JOHN

Those who keep on sinning are against God, for every sin is done against the will of God.

And you know that he became a man so that he could take away our sins, and that there is no sin in him, no missing of God's will at any time in any way. So if we stay close to him, obedient to him, we won't be sinning either. But as for those who keep on sinning, they should realize this: They sin because they have never really known him or become his.

The person who has been born into God's family does not make a practice of sinning, because now God's life is in him. So he can't keep on sinning, for this new life has been born into him and controls him—he has been *born again.*

1 John 3:4-6, 9.

1 JOHN

**Don't always
believe
everything
you hear.**

For there are many false
teachers around, and the way to
find out if their message is from
the Holy Spirit is to ask: Does it
really agree that Jesus Christ,
God's Son, actually became man
with a human body? If so, then
the message is from God. If not,
the message is not from God but
from one who is against Christ,
like the "Antichrist" you have
heard about who is going to
come, and his attitude of enmity
against Christ is already abroad
in the world.

Don't be carried away and
deceived regardless of what they
say. Stand firm and keep a
strong grip on the truth.

1 John 4:1-3. 2 Thessalonians 2:3, 15.

Keep on believing what you have been taught.

If you do, you will always be in close fellowship with both God the Father and his Son. And he himself has promised us this: *eternal life.*

Stay in happy fellowship with the Lord so that when he comes you will be sure that all is well, and will not have to be ashamed and shrink back from meeting him. Since we know that God is always good and does only right, we may rightly assume that all those who do right are his children.

We are already God's children, right now, and we can't even imagine what it is going to be like later on. But we do know this, that when he comes we will be like him, as a result of seeing him as he really is. And everyone who really believes this will try to stay pure because Christ is pure.

1 John 2:24, 25, 28, 29. 1 John 3:2, 3.

2 JOHN

The Truth is in our hearts forever.

God the Father and Jesus Christ his Son will bless us with great mercy and much peace, and with truth and love.

GREAT MERCY:
I have never seen the Lord forsake a man who loves him; nor have I seen the children of the godly go hungry. Instead the godly are able to be generous with their gifts and loans to others, and their children are a blessing.

MUCH PEACE:
Be delighted with the Lord. Then he will give you all your heart's desires. All who humble themselves before the Lord shall be given every blessing and shall have wonderful peace.

WITH TRUTH AND LOVE:
When we obey him, every path he guides us on is fragrant with his lovingkindness and his truth.

2 John 2, 3. Psalm 37:25, 26, 4, 11. Psalm 25:10.

Christians should love one another.

If we love God, we will do whatever he tells us to. And he has told us from the very first to love each other.

Love is very patient and kind, never jealous or envious, never boastful or proud, never haughty or selfish or rude. Love does not demand its own way. It is not irritable or touchy. It does not hold grudges and will hardly even notice when others do it wrong. It is never glad about injustice, but rejoices whenever truth wins out. If you love someone you will be loyal to him no matter what the cost. You will always believe in him, always expect the best of him, and always stand your ground in defending him.

Love goes on forever.

2 John 5, 6. 1 Corinthians 13:4-8.

2 JOHN

Watch out for the false leaders.

There are many of them around—who don't believe that Jesus Christ came to earth as a human being with a body like ours.

Such people are against the truth and against Christ. Beware of being like them, and losing the prize that you and I have been working so hard to get. See to it that you win your full reward from the Lord.

For if you wander beyond the teaching of Christ, you will leave God behind; while if you are loyal to Christ's teachings, you will have God too. Then you will have both the Father and the Son.

If anyone comes to teach you, and he doesn't believe what Christ taught, don't even invite him into your home. Don't encourage him in any way.

2 John 7-10.

3 JOHN

Don't let this bad example influence you.

Proud Diotrephes . . . loves to push himself forward . . . does not admit my authority over him and refuses to listen to me. He not only refuses to welcome the missionary travelers himself, but tells others not to.

There are those who curse their father and mother, and feel themselves faultless despite their many sins.

Follow only what is good. Remember that those who do what is right prove that they are God's children, and those who continue in evil prove that they are far from God.

3 John 11, 9, 10. Proverbs 30:11, 12. 3 John 11.

JUDE

Stay always within the boundaries where God's love can reach and bless you.

Build up your lives ever more strongly upon the foundation of our holy faith, learning to pray in the power and strength of the Holy Spirit.

Wait patiently for the eternal life that our Lord Jesus Christ in his mercy is going to give you.

All glory to him who alone is God, who saves us through Jesus Christ our Lord; yes, splendor and majesty, all power and authority are his from the beginning; his they are and his they ever more shall be.

He is able to keep you from slipping and falling away. Overwhelming victory is ours through Christ who loved us enough to die for us. Nothing can ever separate us from his love.

Jude 21, 20, 21, 24, 25. Romans 8:37, 38.

REVELATION

Sing a new song to the Lord telling about his mighty deeds! For he has won a mighty victory by his power and holiness. He has announced this victory and revealed it to every nation by fulfilling his promise to be kind to Israel. The whole earth has seen God's salvation of his people. That is why the earth breaks out in praise to God, and sings for utter joy!

Sing your praise accompanied by music from the harp. Let the cornets and trumpets shout! Make a joyful symphony before the Lord, the King! Let the sea in all its vastness roar with praise! Let the earth and all those living on it shout, "Glory to the Lord."

Let the waves clap their hands in glee, and the hills sing out their songs of joy before the Lord, for he is coming to judge the world with perfect justice.

Psalm 98:1-9.

Make a joyful symphony before the Lord your King.

REVELATION

**I know that
my Redeemer lives,
and that
he will stand
upon the earth
at last.**

When he comes
we will be like him, as
a result of seeing him as he really is.
We can see and understand only a
little about God now, as if we were
peering at his reflection in a poor
mirror, but someday we are going to
see him in his completeness, face to
face. Now all that I know is hazy and
blurred, but then I will see everything
clearly, just as clearly as God sees into
my heart right now.
No mere man has ever seen, heard
or even imagined what wonderful
things God has ready for those who
love the Lord.

Job 19:25. 1 John 3:2. 1 Corinthians 13:12.
1 Corinthians 2:9.

REVELATION

Looking forward to God's promise of new heavens and a new earth.

For see, I (God) am creating new heavens and a new earth—so wonderful that no one will even think about the old ones anymore.

There are many homes up there where my Father lives, and I am going to prepare them for your coming.

For on that day thorns and thistles, sin, death and decay—the things that overcame the world against its will at God's command—will all disappear, and the world around us will share in the glorious freedom from sin which God's children enjoy.

2 Peter 3:13. Isaiah 65:17. John 14:2. Romans 8:20, 21.

Your eyes will see the King in his beauty, and the highlands of heaven far away.

That wondrous city, the holy Jerusalem ... It was filled with the glory of God, and flashed and glowed like a precious gem, crystal clear like jasper.

No temple could be seen in the city, for the Lord God Almighty and the Lamb are worshiped in it everywhere. And the city has no need of sun or moon to light it, for the glory of God and of the Lamb illuminate it. Its light will light the nations of the earth, and the rulers of the world will come and bring their glory to it.

Its gates never close; they stay open all day long—and there is no night!

Isaiah 33:17. Revelation 21:10, 11, 22-25.

REVELATION

The world staggers like a drunkard.

It shakes like a tent in a storm. It falls
and will not rise again, for the sins of
the earth are very great.
On that day the Lord will punish the
fallen angels in the heavens, and the
proud rulers of the nations on earth.
They will be rounded up like prisoners
and imprisoned in a dungeon until
they are tried and condemned.
Then the Lord of heaven's armies
will mount his throne in Zion and rule
gloriously in Jerusalem, in the sight of
all the elders of his people.
Such glory there will be that all the
brightness of the sun and moon will
seem to fade away. Isaiah 24:20-23.

REVELATION

Satan,
the prince of this world,
shall be cast out.

How you are fallen from heaven, O Lucifer, son of the morning! How you are cut down to the ground—mighty though you were against the nations of the world.

For you said to yourself, "I will ascend to heaven and rule the angels. I will take the highest throne. I will preside on the Mount of Assembly far away in the north. I will climb to the highest heavens and be like the Most High."

But instead, you will be brought down to the pit of hell, down to its lowest depths.

Your heart was filled with pride because of all your beauty. You corrupted your wisdom for the sake of your splendor.

The Lord hates . . . haughtiness.

John 12:31. Isaiah 14:12-15. Ezekiel 28:17. Proverbs 6:16.

DECEMBER 28
REVELATION

The wicked shall be sent away to hell, this is the fate of all the nations forgetting the Lord.

The Evil Creature was captured, and with him the False Prophet. Both of them—the Evil Creature and his False Prophet—were thrown alive into the Lake of Fire that burns with sulphur.

The devil ... will ... be thrown into the Lake of Fire burning with sulphur where the Creature and False Prophet are, and they will be tormented day and night forever and ever.

That is the way it will be at the end of the world—the angels will come and separate the wicked people from the godly, casting the wicked into the fire; there shall be weeping and gnashing of teeth.

Let this encourage God's people to endure patiently every trial and persecution, for they are his saints who remain firm to the end in obedience to his commands and trust in Jesus.

Psalm 9:17. Revelation 19:20. Revelation 20:10. Matthew 13:49, 50. Revelation 14:12.

I am with you always, even to the end of the world.

God is our refuge and strength, a tested help in times of trouble. And so we need not fear even if the world blows up, and the mountains crumble into the sea. Let the oceans roar and foam; let the mountains tremble!

We will have wonderful new bodies in heaven, homes that will be ours forevermore, made for us by God himself, and not by human hands.

For this world is not our home. We are looking forward to our everlasting home in heaven.

And those who are wise—the people of God—shall shine as brightly as the sun's brilliance, and those who turn many to righteousness will glitter like stars forever.

Matthew 28:20. Psalm 46:1-3. 2 Corinthians 5:1. Hebrews 13:14. Daniel 12:3.

AMEN!
COME,
LORD JESUS!

Yes, the Lord God is coming with
mighty power. He will rule with
awesome strength.

While you are waiting for these
things to happen, and for him to
come, try hard to live without sinning;
and be at peace with everyone so that
he will be pleased with you when he
returns.

I would have you learn this great
fact: that a life of doing right is the
wisest life there is. If you live that kind
of life, you'll not limp or stumble as
you run.

He is able . . . to bring you sinless
and perfect, into his glorious presence
with mighty shouts of everlasting joy.
Amen.

Revelation 22:20. Isaiah 40:10. 2 Peter 3:14.
Proverbs 4:11, 12. Jude 25.

Hallelujah! Yes, Praise the Lord!

Praise him in his Temple, and in the
heavens he made with mighty power.
Praise him for his mighty works. Praise
his unequaled greatness.
Praise him with the trumpet and
with lute and harp. Praise him with the
tambourines and processional. Praise
him with stringed instruments and
horns. Praise him with the cymbals,
yes, loud clanging cymbals.
Let everything alive give praises to
the Lord! **You** praise him!
HALLELUJAH!

Psalm 150:1-6.

JANUARY'S
JUBILANT
JOURNAL

_____

_____

_____

_____

_____

_____

_____

_____

_____

_____

_____

_____

_____

_____

_____

_____

_____

_____

_____

FEBRUARY'S
FOREMOST
FEATURES

_____

_____

_____

_____

_____

_____

_____

_____

_____

_____

_____

_____

_____

_____

_____

_____

_____

_____

_____

MARCH'S
MEMORABLE
MOMENTS

_____

_____

_____

_____

_____

_____

_____

_____

_____

_____

_____

_____

_____

_____

_____

_____

_____

_____

APRIL'S
ABUNDANT
ANTICS

_____

_____

_____

_____

_____

_____

_____

_____

_____

_____

_____

_____

_____

_____

_____

_____

_____

_____

_____

_____
_____
_____
_____
_____
_____
_____
_____
_____
_____
_____
_____
_____
_____
_____
_____
_____
_____
_____

JUNE'S
JABBERING
JARGON

_____
_____
_____
_____
_____
_____
_____
_____
_____
_____
_____
_____
_____
_____
_____
_____
_____
_____
_____
_____

JULY'S
JAZZY
JOTTINGS

_____

_____

_____

_____

_____

_____

_____

_____

_____

_____

_____

_____

_____

_____

_____

_____

_____

_____

_____

_____

_____

AUGUST'S
AMIABLE
ADVENTURES

_____

_____

_____

_____

_____

_____

_____

_____

_____

_____

_____

_____

_____

_____

_____

_____

_____

_____

_____

_____

_____

_____

_____

_____

_____

_____

_____

_____

_____

_____

_____

_____

_____

_____

_____

OCTOBER'S
ORIGINAL
OPINIONS

_____

_____

_____

_____

_____

_____

_____

_____

_____

_____

_____

_____

_____

_____

_____

_____

_____

_____

_____

_____
_____
_____
_____
_____
_____
_____
_____
_____
_____
_____
_____
_____
_____
_____
_____
_____
_____
_____
_____
_____

DECEMBER'S
DYNAMIC
DETAILS

_____

_____

_____

_____

_____

_____

_____

_____

_____

_____

_____

_____

_____

_____

_____

_____

_____

_____

_____

_____

_____

Kudos to

Hildegard Adler: August 3
Gene Ahrens: January 1, April 3, August 10, December 21
Tim Botts: July 11, September 23
Paul Brackley: February 8, 17, May 22, October 31
Paul Buddle: January 11, February 25, April 22, May 5, 16, July 9, 31,
    August 1, October 21, November 17, December 31
Ron Byers: April 23, December 25
Mike Chiaverina: February 10
Ron Engh: March 26, July 20
Marc R. Francis: February 1
Michael Goldberg: August 15, October 4, November 3
Kent Halsell: May 30
Margarite Hoefler: October 1
Grant Heilman: May 26-27, July 13, November 2
Gary Irving: August 26
William Koechling: March 31, June 4, October 3, November 10, 15,
    December 26
Harold M. Lambert: July 29
Courtesy of LEGO Systems, Inc.: March 11
Jean-Claude Lejeune: November 13
Robert McKendrick: January 17, February 5, 23-24, March 9, April 24,
    May 17, 20, 24, June 1, 21, August 31-September 1, September 15,
    October 7, 18
Robert Meier: March 6
Jonathan A. Meyers: January 7, March 17, 23, April 6, 11, June 5, 9,
    August 18, September 20, October 16, 28, November 7, 23
Paul Mouw: July 1
R. Mullin: November 28
NASA: January 2, August 27
William S. Nawrocki: August 11
Roger Neal: March 14, April 15, July 5, September 3, 16, December 20
Neal Nicolay: April 5, 26, June 19, July 14
Regis Nicoll: May 8
NOAA: January 18
Duane H. Patten: February 19
Kenneth C. Poertner: January 25, March 12
H. Armstrong Roberts: January 8, August 4
Rich Rosenkoetter: December 8
Will and Angie Rumpf: January 26
James L. Shaffer: April 9, 19, 27, June 11, 17, 27, July 26, September 14, 27,
    October 11-12, November 11-12, 16, 30, December 6, 29
Florence Sharp: January 14